Seeing Jesus

Social Justice Activities for Today Based on Matthew 25

PHYLLIS VOS WEZEMAN

The Pastoral Center

Dedication

To Jennifer Spencer Pitcher ...

... a friend who uses her talent, time, and treasure—personally and professionally—in ministry to the hungry, thirsty, stranger, poor, sick, and imprisoned. P.V.W.

Acknowledgments

Colleen Aalsburg Wiessner
(February 6, 1954—August 5, 2009)

In loving tribute to Colleen, *Seeing Jesus* is Phyllis' timely, yet timeless, revision of the out-of-print book *When Did We See You? Sixty Creative Activities to Help Fourth to Eighth Graders Recognize Jesus Today* (Wezeman, Phyllis Vos and Colleen Aalsburg Wiessner. Notre Dame, IN: Ave Maria Press, 1994). Colleen was an extraordinarily gifted educator and Assistant Professor in the Department of Adult and Higher Education at North Carolina State University. May her legacy live on as readers are challenged to use their gifts to serve others.

Thanks to Kenneth R. Wezeman for writing the Bible Background on Matthew 25:31-46 for this resource.

We are grateful to Ave Maria Press for permission to use illustrations that appeared in the original edition of this book.

ISBN 978-1-949628-23-4
Printed in the United States of America.
10 9 8 7 6 5 4 3 2 1   22 21 20 19

TABLE OF CONTENTS

Introduction _____5

Bible Background _____7

I Was Hungry _____9

Working for Justice. 12
Dispelling the Myths 14
Hungering for Happiness 18
Setting the Example 22
Recognizing the Hungry 30
Caring through Prayer. 35
Sharing Your Resources. 38
Multiplying the Food 43
Remembering the Hungry 45
Spreading the Word 47

I Was Thirsty _____51

Thirsting for God 54
Appreciating Water 57
Quenching a Thirst. 60
Discovering Water Facts 63
Refreshing Water Themes 74
Praising God for Water 77
Exploring Pollution Problems 80
Living Water 83

Flowing with Justice. 86
Filling a Cup in Jesus' Name 89

I Was a Stranger _____91

Displaying Hospitality 94
Welcoming New Neighbors 96
Putting Out the Welcome Mat 100
Talking at Home 102
Engaging Others. 105
Singing the Language of Love. 108
Offering a Prayer 111
Showing Kindness to All 113
Blessing a Stranger 115
Making New Friends 119

I Was Poor _____121

Clothing the Poor. 123
Expressing the Pain 125
Becoming Personally Involved. 127
Searching for Support 130
Encouraging through Music. 133
Addressing Unemployment 135
Giving for the Poor. 138
Celebrating the Caring 141
Responding to Needs. 143
Helping the Homeless 145

I Was Sick _____ 147

Sending a Caring Message 150
Identifying the Feelings. 152
Focusing on Feelings 154
Meeting Special Needs. 158
Creating Recipes for Healthy Living 161
Uplifting the Sick 165
Proclaiming the Message. 172
Ministering In Mercy. 175
Taking Care of the Sick 179
Portraying Health Issues 181

I Was Imprisoned _____ 183

Spreading Some Sunshine. 185
Suffering for Their Beliefs 187
Breaking Down Walls 189
Overcoming the Bonds of Materialism. . 191

Learning about Literacy 193
Unlocking the Fears. 197
Hiding in a Secret Prison 199
Reading about Addictions. 202
Touching with Love 205
Feeling Trapped by Abuse. 208

Bibliography _____ 211

Resources _____ 213

Methods _____ 214

Scripture _____ 219

About the Author _____225

INTRODUCTION

Who are the **hungry**?

Could she be the elderly woman living down the street who can no longer get to the market on her own?

Who are the **thirsty**?

Can he be the young adolescent yearning for God to help him make sense of his life?

Who is the **stranger**?

Could she be the new girl at school who has just moved to the area with her family?

Who are the **poor**?

Would they be the people whose home and possessions were destroyed in the overnight fire?

Who are the **sick**?

Could he be the teenager who seeks to control his low self-image by eating the wrong foods?

Who are the **imprisoned**?

Might she be the young girl suffering from the pain of physical abuse?

Jesus concluded a long discourse recorded in the gospel of Matthew with a parable of a king who judged his subjects based on how they treated one another. In fact, the king told his people, "Truly I tell you, just as you did it to one of the least of these who are members of my family, you did it to me." Christians have always taken this to mean that by sharing God's love with the "least of these," they are doing it for Jesus.

The difficulty in this teaching often comes in identifying the least ones. Generally, the words seems so abstract. Who actually knows a person who is physically hungry? Who is acquainted with someone who has been jailed? By looking at these six questions in a new light, the participants will be helped to a clearer understanding of who these people are and how to help meet their needs. The learners will also realize that everyone comes into daily contact with someone in one or more of these categories and that, from time to time, they may also fit some of these classifications. Through recognizing the least of these, meeting their needs, and sharing God's love, the young people will find out what it is like to come face to face with Jesus Christ.

Called the parable of the last judgment, the story of the king and his subjects is only fifteen verses long, yet Matthew 25:31-46 provides a concise synopsis of themes such as justice, love in action, and faithfulness which are woven throughout the Bible. Even the location of this passage makes an important point. In the same discourse, Jesus also shares the parable of the ten bridesmaids, a message that reminds his followers of his imminent return, and the parable of the talents, which tells Christians that their God-given talents must be multiplied for the good of others and of God's kingdom. In both parables we are told how to use our time before Jesus returns.

In Matthew 25:31-46, Jesus is even more specific. He presents a clear model of discipleship. We are reminded that Christ is always with us, sometimes disguised as those around us who need our help. Most importantly, these are not tasks for the highly skilled or the uniquely called, they are something which every follower can and must do in the name of Christ. Since Jesus would no longer be on earth with the disciples, he wanted to make it clear that good deeds done for others were the same as kindnesses expressed directly to him.

The six chapters of *Seeing Jesus* each contain 10 learning activities which explore one aspect of the chapter's theme. Each lesson plan is organized into three parts: Learn, Locate, and Lead. Learn presents a short description of the theme of the activity and describes what the students will do. Locate provides a list of supplies and preparations needed in order to present the learning experience. Lead details the directions for successfully guiding a group through the design. Although each lesson is related to the passage, Matthew 25:31-46, it is also organized around another story or verse from the Bible which further illustrates the specific topic.

Sharing God's love was a task not only given to the disciples thousands of years ago, it is the responsibility of every Christian in any age. *Seeing Jesus* provides creative, concrete methods for responding to Jesus' commission. It once again challenges each and every learner with the question, "What will you do?"

BIBLE BACKGROUND

Matthew 25:31-46

The Gospel of Matthew was written for a Jewish audience. This is evident in many ways. Matthew opens with a genealogy that demonstrates that Jesus descended from Abraham and, furthermore, that he was in the line of David, the great King of Israel. Already in the second chapter, the story of the magi is presented to demonstrate that Jesus was born to be the King. The theme of the kingship of Jesus continues throughout the book. For example, when Matthew tells the story of Jesus' triumphal entry into Jerusalem, he takes care to point out that the prophet Zechariah said that the King would come meek and riding on a donkey. In the Matthew 25 passage, verse 34, Jesus, who often referred to himself as the "Son of Man," equates the "Son of Man" with the "King."

Furthermore, as the gospel unfolds, there are many references to Old Testament prophecies and quotations from the Old Testament with which only a Jewish audience would be intimately familiar. Matthew takes great care to show how prophecy is fulfilled in Jesus and his ministry. In chapter 2, Matthew says that the murder of innocent children ordered by Herod, as well as the return from the flight into Egypt, are fulfillment of prophecy. The theme of fulfillment of prophecy occurs in other passages, e.g. 13:14, 35 and 26:56. The message is clear that Jesus is the Messiah and King promised in prophecy.

In the chapters leading up to Matthew 25, Jesus clearly stands in judgment over the hypocrisy of the Pharisees. As Messiah and King, he has every right to do so. When asked what the greatest commandment is (22:36) Jesus responds that it is to love God completely, and a second commandment is to "love your neighbor as yourself." [Looking back at the Ten Commandments that structure is obvious already in Exodus 20. There the Lord says he loved Israel— "brought you out of the land of Egypt"— so Israel should love the Lord and one another.] Jesus criticizes the Pharisees for keeping commandments so that they will be praised and admired for their piety while lacking love for their neighbors. They are only "actors" playing a role. (Ὑποκριτής = hypocrite, the Greek word meaning actor.) They put on the "mask" of the Greek theater to look pious, but they have no real piety. They speak the proper theological language, but it doesn't affect their hearts. Their actions show no love for their neighbors. So, Jesus goes on to justly pronounce condemnation on their actions in chapter 23.

Jesus then begins a discourse on the end of this age. He describes the end times in chapter 24. That brings us to the focus of our passage. In Matthew 25 he describes the coming of the Son of Man with his angels at the end of time. He will sit on his throne and separate the sheep from the goats. The sheep are those with true piety. The goats are the "actors." The goats will be shown to be pretending while the sheep have real faith, the ones who have been changed by God's love. They are the ones who saw their neighbor in need and helped. They are the ones who demonstrate their faith in their love for others.

When we feed the hungry, give a drink to the thirsty, offer hospitality to the stranger, clothe those exposed to the elements, minister to the sick, or visit the imprisoned, we are demonstrating that the love God has shown us has affected our hearts. The apostle John sums up Jesus' message succinctly when he says, "Dear friends, since God loved us, we also ought to love one another" (1 John 4:11).

I WAS HUNGRY

Over and over again the Bible tells of God's concern for those who are hungry. At creation God provided everything people needed in order to live. It is only after Adam and Eve sinned that people had to struggle to survive and to work hard to meet their needs. Isaiah 55:1 proclaims the day when people will be able to come, buy, and eat ... without money and without price. The image of heaven as a banquet reveals God's ideal. Even the poor, the lame, and the outcast will have a place at God's table.

Throughout salvation history God provided food for people in miraculous ways. Manna in the wilderness, Exodus 16:4-35, and the feeding of the 5,000, Mark 6:34-44, are just two examples. God also provided food through faithful servants who put love into action and cared for those who were hungry. They were commended for their justice and kindness. In the parable of the last judgment, Matthew 25:40, Jesus said of these people, 'Just as you did it to one of the least of these who are members of my family, you did it to me.'

This chapter considers three types of hunger which are present both in biblical stores and in the world today. The activities in this chapter will help the participants explore causes, effects, and solutions of physical, emotional, and spiritual hunger. They will discover what it means to feed those who are hungry, meeting their needs in the name of Jesus.

Chart

Title	Scripture	Theme	Activity/Method	Page
Overview	► Exodus 16:4-35 ► Isaiah 55:1 ► Matthew 6:34-44 ► Matthew 25:35a, 36b, 37a, 42a, 44a ► Matthew 25:40	► Hunger		9
Working for Justice	► Psalm 146:7	► Hunger Relief Organizations	► Banners/Textiles: Brown Paper Bag Banner	12
Dispelling the Myths	► Matthew 12:1-8	► Hunger Myths and Realities	► Creative Writing: Fairy Tales	14
Hungering for Happiness	► Matthew 5:6	► Hunger for Happiness	► Drama: Talk Show	18
Setting the Example	► Genesis 1:29-31 ► Genesis 18:1-8 ► Genesis 45:16-24 ► Genesis 47:13-17 ► Exodus 13:3-10 ► Ruth 2:1-16 ► 2 Samuel 9 ► 1 Kings 17:8-16 ► 1 Kings 19:1-15 ► 2 Kings 4:42-44 ► Daniel 1:8-17 ► Matthew 8:14-15 ► Matthew 12:1-8 ► Matthew 25:35-40 ► Matthew 26:17-29 ► Luke 10:29-37 ► Luke 12:15-21 ► Luke 14:15-24 ► Luke 16:19-31 ► John 6:1-14	► Biblical and Contemporary Hunger Situations	► Game: Biblical Situation Cards and Contemporary Situation Cards	22

	► John 21:4-14 ► Acts 2:43-47 ► Acts 6:1-7 ► Acts 16:11-15 ► James 2:14-17			
Recognizing the Hungry	► Isaiah 58:10 ► Matthew 25:35-45	► Hunger Awareness and Action	► Dance/Gesture/Movement: Gestural Interpretation ► Music: Song - "I Was Hungry"	30
Caring through Prayer	► John 21:4-18	► Emotional Hunger	► Art: Cut Outs/Prayers ► Storytelling: Feed My Sheep	35
Sharing Your Resources	► John 15:13	► Sacrificial Giving	► Puppetry: Brown Paper Grocery Bag Body Puppet ► Storytelling: "The Rabbit In the Moon"	38
Multiplying the Food	► Matthew 14:13-21 ► Mark 6:31-55 ► Luke 9:12-17 ► John 6:1-14	► Feeding the 5,000	► Storytelling: Rhythm Story - "Multiplying the Food"	43
Remembering the Hungry	► Matthew 6:11	► Daily Bread/ The Lord's Prayer ► Hunger Reminder	► Art: Wooden Spoon	45
Spreading the Word	► Luke 16:19-31	► World Food Distribution	► Art: Bread Symbols/Actions ► Creative Writing: Litany ► Culinary: Breads of the World	47

Working for Justice

Psalm 146:7

**Happy are those who
execute justice for the oppressed;
who give food to the hungry.**

Learn

Participants will discover ways people help to feed the hungry and create a banner to advertise a need or a program related to this theme.

Locate

- Bags, boxes, and wrappers from food
- Bags, brown paper or burlap, or a piece of natural colored burlap
- Bible
- Glue
- Information on one or more food programs
- Labels from cans and jars
- Markers, dark colors
- Scissors
- Tape

Lead

There are many ways in which we can live the words of Psalm 146:7: execute justice for the oppressed and give food to the hungry. Hunger programs of parishes, organizations, and schools are supported through the efforts of people who give food, money, and time. However, many people still need to know how they can help to feed those in need. In this activity the participants will learn some of the ways Christians help to feed the hungry. They will communicate the problem of physical hunger to their local faith community and make a banner to advertise a need or a program related to this theme.

Ask the participants to name ways in which their church, school, or organization helps to feed the hungry. Activities or programs might include the following:

- advertising for volunteers to help in a food bank;
- baking items to raise funds for a hunger program;
- buying canned goods to support a food pantry;
- collecting food for disaster relief;
- filling food baskets;
- gleaning food at local farms;
- harvesting leftover garden foods for distribution or sale;
- hosting a soup supper to raise money for a cause;
- offering food items to a homeless shelter;
- taking a collection for food relief through programs such as the Catholic Relief Services Rice Bowl
- volunteering at a soup kitchen

Next, help the participants understand that there are many steps involving both actions and people which are needed to feed the hungry. Ask the group to suggest ways that food gets from the people who donate it to those who need it. Act out the process with the participants. Set up a chain of people and events which occur in order for the hungry to be fed. This could include, for example:

► people who donate food or money to pay for food;
► people who box or package food to be delivered to a program;
► people who drive food to the program;
► people who provide space for the food to be stored and distributed;
► people who unpack food and organize it for distribution;
► people who distribute the food;
► people who come to the program to receive food which they need;
► people who clean and maintain the distribution center.

Read Psalm 146:7 to the group. Discuss how this verse relates to feeding the hungry. Ask the students what they might do to help people become aware of the hungry in the community and how they could invite more people to help feed those who need food.

Provide information about a local organization and explain some of its specific needs. An agency may request food to distribute, money to purchase special items, or volunteers to work at a site. Invite the group to make a banner to advertise the needs of a local hunger relief organization. Several banners could be made, depending on the number of participants and the variety of hunger programs in which the church is involved.

As a background for the banner, use brown paper grocery bags, a burlap bag, or a piece of burlap which have been taped together. Decorate the banner in one of several ways:

Draw outlines of letters on labels and wrappers using thick, dark-colored markers. Cut out the letters, leaving the dark borders so that the letters will stand out clearly. Tape or glue in place on the banner.

Make a collage using the outer packaging from food. Labels from cans or jars, wrappers, bags, or box surfaces can all be arranged on the banner and then glued or taped in place. Write the message or information in dark permanent marker across the surface of the collage.

Use labels and wrappers to create a border around the edges of the banner. For the message, use more labels or plain paper cut into letters which describe the food program's need.

Provide the materials and allow the group to use them to design a banner. Assign or suggest one of the construction methods, if necessary.

Close the session by gathering in a circle around the completed banner(s). Pray that God will use the artwork to help those who see it reach out and help hungry people. Together, hang the banner(s) in a prominent place in the church or school where it will be seen throughout the week.

Dispelling the Myths

Matthew 12:7
'I desire mercy and not sacrifice.'

Learn

Participants will discover myths and realities about the causes of hunger and write fairy tales to share truths about this topic.

Locate

► Bible

► Copy machine or printer

► Crayons or markers

► Paper for copy machine or printer

► Paper or poster board for presentations

► Pencils or pens

► Resource sheet: "Myths and Realities of Hunger"

► Resources on the myths and realities of hunger

Advance Preparation

► Assemble resource materials on the myths and realities of hunger.

► If desired, invite speakers from agencies that deal with hunger issues.

Lead

It would seem that most people in the world want to do something to combat the problem of hunger. Unfortunately, many people have been misinformed about the causes of this issue which has led to false myths. When these myths are not addressed, people can become complacent and resistant to offer their assistance. In this activity, participants will uncover the differences between myths and realities and write fairy tales to share the truth about causes of hunger.

Tell the participants that there are many common misconceptions, or myths, about world hunger. Explain that exploring some of these widespread, yet only partially valid, beliefs can help people work to address the causes and to end the issue. Distribute a copy of the "Myths and Realities of Hunger" resource sheet to each participant. Assign small groups one myth and reality statement. Direct them to research information on the issue and then report their findings to the class. Remark that those considering each issue could depict the data they find on a chalkboard or a piece of newsprint or poster board to use in their presentation. They could also create a PowerPoint presentation, including pictures, to be projected for the group. In addition, invited speakers from hunger related agencies might work with the teams to present the facts.

Allow time for the students to prepare the data on their assigned myth and reality statements. Offer guidance, as well as encouragement, as needed. Once everyone has completed the task, invite each group to make a presentation. Take time for comments and questions after each talk.

Once the hunger information has been discussed, apply the lesson by inviting the participants to write a fairy tale for each myth and reality. Share the example provided or write a sample with the entire group. Assign individuals or partners to write fairy tales for each of the statements. Distribute paper, pens, and pencils for the project. Share the results with the entire class.

Example

▶ Myth One
There is not enough food for everyone in the world.

Sample Fairy Tale

Once there was a king who loved to eat. One day he wondered, "What if I ate so much that I would run out of all of my favorite foods?" The king decided that would make him very sad. He called together his palace servants and told them to build walls around all of the fields and factories of food. The king commanded the servants to put his seal on the gate in each wall. Although the king continued to share food with his loyal subjects, he made sure that no one else would be able to steal what now belonged to him.

▶ Reality
The world's grain production alone could provide everyone in the world with enough calories and protein for good health. Unfortunately, because people who are hungry are also poor, the grain is not equally or fairly distributed to all nations.

Sample Fairy Tale

Once there was a king who loved to eat. One day he wondered, "What if I ate so much that I would run out of all of my favorite foods?" The king decided that it was not fair for him to have more and better food than everyone else, or to eat so much that others might not have enough food. So, he called together all of his servants and sent them out to see if the subjects of the land had enough to eat. The king began an education program in all of the kingdom to remind people to care about everyone and to be wise about what they ate. Then he called together a meeting of all the other kings of the world to figure out a plan to make sure that there would always be enough food for all of the kingdoms.

After the fairy tales are written, invite volunteers to share their stories with the class. To extend the activity, offer the writers the opportunity to illustrate their fairy tales. Provide crayons and markers. Display the finished projects in the classroom or combine them to form a class book on the myths and realities of hunger.

Myths and Realities of Hunger

Myth One

There is not enough food for everyone in the world.

Reality One

The world's grain production alone could provide everyone in the world with enough calories and protein for good health. Unfortunately, because people who are hungry are also poor, the grain is not equally or fairly distributed to all nations.

Myth Two

There isn't enough suitable land for farming.

Reality Two

Unfortunately, much potential farm land is uncultivated or inefficiently used. In many countries with widespread hunger, a few land owners control nearly all agricultural production. Their land is sometimes used for cash crops such as coffee or cotton instead of food. In many places, one harvest is gathered per year when there could be two or three. In some areas, valuable farmland is being paved over to build more houses and businesses. Other acreage is damaged by erosion or overgrazing.

Myth Three

There are too many people to feed.

Reality Three

Overpopulation is not the cause of hunger. Actually, just the opposite is true. Many poor families have a large number of children in the hope that some will survive to work in the fields or in the city to add to the family's income.

Myth Four

Hunger is the result of natural disasters.

Reality Four

In some areas, hunger can be directly traced to floods, droughts, and other natural disasters. Yet, starvation is also common in many other parts of the world where no natural disasters have occurred.

Myth Five

Modern, large-scale agriculture is the answer.

Reality Five

Small farmers don't have the money to invest in machinery, fuels, and fertilizers. In less developed countries, reliance on machines may actually displace workers, thus adding to the hunger problem by taking away people's sources of income. Many studies have shown that small farms actually produce more food per acre than large farms.

Myth Six

People are lazy.

Reality Six

Nobody wants to starve. In countries where unemployment and illiteracy are widespread, jobs are not available for many people. Therefore, many hungry people do not have money to buy food.

Myth Seven

Growing more food will mean less hunger in poor countries.

Reality Seven

Until a more equitable method for distributing food between rich and poor nations is established, it does not matter how much more food is grown. Sometimes excess food never makes it to the hungry ones.

Myth Eight

Hunger is a contest between rich countries and poor countries.

Reality Eight

It must be acknowledged that, rich or poor, all people of the world are part of the same global food system. Food is gradually coming under the control of a few huge corporations that grow and market food for the benefit of people who have money to buy it. People in poor countries pay food prices that are determined by what people in rich countries are willing to pay. Even in rich countries, small farmers find themselves unable to afford the machinery they need, and people on fixed incomes cannot afford to pay high prices for the food they must have to survive.

Myth Nine

More foreign monetary aid must be provided to poorer nations.

Reality Nine

Unfortunately, foreign aid is not always used to develop a country's ability to feed hungry citizens and it might be used for other purposes such as defense.

Myth Ten

People will eat anything they are given.

Reality Ten

In some countries and cultures people have strict dietary practices and principles. There are certain foods they cannot and will not eat.

Adapted from:

Lappe, Frances Moore and Joseph Collins. *World Hunger: Twelve Myths.* New York, NY: Grove Press, 1998.

Hungering for Happiness

Matthew 5:6

'Blessed are those who hunger and thirst for righteousness, for they will be filled.'

Learn

Participants will explore the theme of hungering for happiness by creating and presenting a television-style talk show.

Locate

- ► Bible
- ► Chairs or stools
- ► Clipboard
- ► Copy machine or printer
- ► Markers
- ► Microphone for prop
- ► Paper for copy machine or printer
- ► Poster board
- ► Props for commercials (optional)
- ► Props for set such as lamp, plant, rug, and/or table (optional)
- ► Resource sheet: "Talk Show Questions"

Advance Preparation

- ► Prepare a sign for the game show, such as a logo and a name, by drawing a design and writing words on poster board.
- ► Reproduce the Talk Show Questions for people who will play the parts.

Lead

In the words of the fifth Beatitude, Matthew 5:6, Jesus explained that some people hunger for happiness much in the same way that others hunger for food. Unfortunately, many individuals seek to find happiness in ways that will never completely satisfy them. In the Sermon on the Mount, Jesus explained that blessed or happy people are those who hunger and thirst for righteousness. They are the ones who will be filled. In this activity, the participants will create and present a television-style talk show that discusses many different ways that people search for happiness. They will discover some of the ways that God provides happiness to those who experience a hunger to do what is right.

Begin by reading the scripture verse for this session, Matthew 5:6, to the class. Ask the learners to explain the meaning of the word "righteousness." If necessary, add information to enhance the definition. For example, righteousness means acting in a just, upright manner; doing what is good, right, or proper. It means seeking to do what God wants us to do. Tell the group that being right with God is a brief way of remembering the meaning of righteousness.

Talk about the contrast of hungering and thirsting for righteousness and the kind of hungering and thirsting which is heard on many radio programs or seen on numerous television stations, especially on talk shows. Ask the students if they have ever listened to or watched morning, afternoon, or evening talk shows. Allow the group to name as many of these types of programs as they can recall in a few minutes. Ask the students why they think there are so many of these kinds of shows. Mention some of the hopeless dilemmas and life situations that are presented on these programs. Compare the hunger and thirst for righteousness to the hunger and thirst which is often seen on talk shows. Allow time for discussion.

Tell the group that they are going to produce their own television-type talk show. The topic of the program will be the search for happiness. The name of the show, or a promotional teaser, could be "I'll Be Happy If … Seekers of Happiness Tell Stories about the Search!" Of course, the group can suggest its own title for the production. Assign roles like host(s), guests, crew, and members of the audience. One or more group members, or a leader or teacher, can serve as the host, interviewing a number of guests playing different parts. Each guest will be seeking happiness in a specific way, such as through education, fame, friends, fun, possessions, money, or travel. Determine the specific topic for each talk show guest. If there are additional members of the class, assign them parts as crew or audience members.

Allow time for preparation. Distribute the questions to the guests and guide them as they decide how they will respond to them.

While the guests are working, the hosts should prepare their presentation, too. In between each guest, the host can make an announcement setting up the audience for the next speaker. They can use statements like, "Coming up next, On the Fast Track: Happiness through Success," to form a bridge between the guest appearances.

During the preparation period, members of the audience could plan commercial breaks for the show. These should relate to a product or experience which offers happiness. Possible topics include vacation

spots to enjoy, loans to help people afford the things they want, products which make folks feel happier about their appearance, and entertainment opportunities.

While the host, guests, and audience members are working on their parts, have the crew create a set for the show. Comfortable chairs or stools can be used for a setting in which the host and guest will talk. All guests can sit in chairs in front, or guests can be called to come up one at a time. Commercial breaks may be used as a time to re-arrange people. Provide a prop microphone for the host. Other props, such as a lamp, plant, rug, or table could be added to make the set attractive for the show. A sign with the name of the show may serve as a background.

Once the hosts, guests, commercial-makers, and production crew have completed their tasks, talk about the role of the audience. The audience will be made up of any group members who are not doing their presentation at that time. Therefore, participants will be playing more than one role during the talk show production. The audience can challenge the guests to look in other places for happiness. Perhaps a call-in guest could be prepared to help explain how the guests will find real happiness. Members of the audience could explain ways in which God has helped them to feel happy. Make sure the students do not give simplistic solutions to very deep voids which so many people feel in their lives. Explain that it is not helpful to quickly say, "God will take care of it," to people who are searching for meaning. Audience members may also tell ways in which they struggled in similar situations and what helped them in the process.

Present the talk show. The host should ask each guest how the thing they are seeking can or cannot provide happiness. Each interview might end with the question, "Are you happy?" Instruct each guest to answer that question with the phrase, "No, not yet, but I'll keep trying." Ask the students to stay in their roles throughout the show as much as possible. Assist the participants throughout the production to help things flow as smoothly as possible.

After the production, discuss the experience with the participants. Pass the prop microphone around and let each person respond individually to questions like "What did you learn from doing the production?" or "What advice would you give to people who are searching for happiness?" Remind the students of the need to seek God in all decisions.

Close the session with a guided prayer. Suggest a topic and allow time so each person can silently pray about it. If desired, begin the prayer with a few general petitions of thanksgiving to God. Then proceed with the response, "Lord, hear our prayer." Lead the group in praying for some or all of the following things:

► We thank you for the things which we learned today.

► We pray for the many people who are hungering for happiness.

► Please help to satisfy the people who are hungering for happiness.

► Please help me to look for happiness in the right places.

► Thank you for the happiness you provide.

End the prayer by saying, "Thank you that you always hear and answer our prayers. Amen."

If desired, present the talk show for one or more additional groups. Possible settings include a church potluck, a youth group meeting, or a Sunday School class. Parents, as well as younger or older students, will all benefit from seeing the show. In addition, the production group will learn more each time it is offered.

Talk Show Questions

Choose any or all of the following questions to ask the guests.

▸ Why did you think _____ would make you happy?

▸ Did _____ provide happiness?

▸ Describe your quest to search for happiness through _____.

▸ Tell us three ways that you are happier because of _____.

Setting the Example

Genesis 47:13

Now there was no food in all the land, for the famine was very severe. The land of Egypt and the land of Canaan languished because of the famine.

Learn

Participants will play a game to learn about biblical people who helped the hungry and to respond to contemporary situations involving people who need food.

Locate

▶ Bags, brown paper grocery type

▶ Bags, cans, and packages of food

▶ Bibles

▶ Copy machine or printer

▶ Paper cutter or scissors

▶ Paper for copy machine or printer, 2 colors

▶ Resource sheet: "Bible Situation Game Cards"

▶ Resource sheet: "Contemporary Situation Game Cards"

▶ Tables

Advance Preparation

▶ Arrange to gather enough food to fill at least one large paper grocery bag per small group. Announce ahead of time that participants should bring one or two food items to class to donate to people in need.

▶ Duplicate the Bible Situation Game Cards and the Contemporary Situation Game Cards resource sheets on two different colors of paper. Cut the cards apart and stack each set in a different pile. Be sure to prepare a set of both types of cards for each table.

▶ Set up a table for each small group of four to six participants. Place a paper grocery bag; a variety of bags, boxes, and cans of food; a Bible; and the two decks of cards on each table.

Lead

In the Bible there are many Old Testament and New Testament stories of people who fed the hungry. Genesis 47:13-17, the account of Joseph, is an example of how God rescued a family by satisfying their physical and spiritual hungers. In this lesson, the participants will use a game format to read about biblical people and discover ways they fed others. Players will encounter contemporary situations related to hunger and decide how to respond to needs. The activity will also help learners understand how their lives can be examples for others to follow.

As the participants arrive, seat four to six people around each table. Read Genesis 47:13-17 to the group. Remark that this is a story of what Joseph did to help hungry people. Tell the class that they will play a game to discover other examples of people in the Bible who fed the hungry. In addition, they will decide what people today, including themselves, can do to assist those in need of food.

Explain that the object of the game is to fill a grocery bag with the food items on their table. This is accomplished by taking turns and working cooperatively to answer questions. To begin the game, a player may choose a card from either pile. One set of cards describes biblical situations in which people were fed and the other stack suggests contemporary situations related to hunger issues. The player who picked the card attempts to answer the question. If it is a Bible Situation, the player can state the answer or look up the verse before responding. A contemporary card may have several answers and the player may offer all ideas that come to mind. After the player has had an opportunity to answer, other players can add ideas or suggestions. Each time a question is answered the player who picked the card chooses a food item to place in the grocery bag. Everyone wins when the bag is filled. Note that players should alternate picking cards from opposite decks, for example, if the first player picks from the Bible Situation stack, the second player should select from the Contemporary Situation pile.

Continue playing the game until the grocery bag is filled with food items. Emphasize that everyone wins when people share what they have with others. Decide as a group what to do with the bag(s) of food. After the decision is made, form a circle around the bag or bags and pray for those who will receive the food.

Answers- Bible Situation Cards

Old Testament

1. Eden
2. Abraham, Sarah
3. Joseph
4. Moses
5. Ruth
6. Mephibosheth
7. meal, oil
8. angel
9. Elisha, 100
10. Daniel

New Testament

1. She was healed
2. Grain field/Grain
3. Him
4. Remembrance
5. A Samaritan
6. Storing food
7. The poor
8. Lazarus
9. 5,000
10. Shore
11. The needy
12. Deacons
13. Lydia
14. Faith, Works

Bible Situation Game Cards (1/3)

Bible Situation – Old Testament #1

God provided everything Adam and Eve would need to eat in order to survive. It was all in a garden called _____. Check it out: Genesis 1:29-31

Bible Situation – Old Testament #2

_____ saw three strangers traveling toward him in the desert. He and _____ welcomed them and fed them a meal. Check it out: Genesis 18:1-8.

Bible Situation – Old Testament #3

_____ gave grain to his brothers and to many others during a famine which kept them from growing food. Check it out: Genesis 45:16-24.

Bible Situation – Old Testament #4

This great leader named _____ helped the people of God celebrate the Passover with a special meal so that they would always remember how God set them free from slavery. Check it out: Exodus 13:3-10.

Bible Situation – Old Testament #5

Boaz let _____ glean the extra grain in the fields. He fed her a meal and also told his workers to leave some extra grain for her. Check it out: Ruth 2:1-16.

Bible Situation – Old Testament #6

David invited _____ to eat at his table because he was the son of David's friend Jonathan. This was unusual because _____ was crippled and came from the family who fought against David. Check it out: 2 Samuel 9.

Bible Situation – Old Testament #7

A widow shared her last _____ and _____ with Elijah. A miracle occurred and she and her son did not run out of food for many days. Check it out: 1 Kings 17:8-16.

Bible Situation – Old Testament #8

Elijah was so sad he sat under a tree and decided to die. God sent an _____ to encourage him and to bring him food. Check it out: 1 Kings 19:1-15.

Bible Situation Game Cards (2/3)

Bible Situation – Old Testament #9

A man gave twenty loaves of barley bread and fresh grain to _____ to thank God for providing food for him. _____ used it to feed _____ people and there was some left over. Check it out: 2 Kings 4:42-44.

Bible Situation – Old Testament #10

_____ refused to eat the "junk food" offered to him by King Nebuchadnezzar's servant. He chose, instead, to eat the healthy food he knew would be good for him and would please God. Check it out: Daniel 1:8-17.

Bible Situation – New Testament #1

Peter's mother-in-law got up and prepared a meal for Jesus and his followers right after _____. Check it out: Matthew 8:14-15.

Bible Situation – New Testament #2

Jesus and his followers were hungry. Passing through a _____ they picked _____ to eat. They were criticized for working on the Sabbath. Jesus said it is more important to feed the hungry and to show kindness than to follow rules that are not compassionate. Check it out: Matthew 12:1-8.

Bible Situation – New Testament #3

Jesus said whenever you fed the least of these, you did it to _____. Check it out: Matthew 25:35-40.

Bible Situation – New Testament #4

Jesus fed his disciples a final meal before he died. Why? _____. Check it out: Matthew 26:17-29.

Bible Situation – New Testament #5

_____ paid an innkeeper to feed and take care of an injured man until he recovered from being mugged. Check it out: Luke 10:29-37.

Bible Situation – New Testament #6

Jesus warned against _____ instead of sharing it with others and being generous to God. Check it out: Luke 12:15-21.

Bible Situation Game Cards (3/3)

Bible Situation - New Testament #7 A person prepared a huge banquet and invited many friends to share it. When they were too busy to come _____ were invited to eat it instead. Check it out: Luke 14:15-24.	**Bible Situation - New Testament #8** The rich man refused to share food with the poor man _____. What happened? Check it out: Luke 16:19-31.
Bible Situation - New Testament #9 A young boy shared his lunch of five loaves and two fish. Jesus used it to feed a hungry crowd of _____ people. Check it out: John 6:1-14.	**Bible Situation - New Testament #10** The disciples had fished all night without catching anything. Jesus told them to cast their nets on the other side. They caught more than the boat could hold. Then Jesus fed them breakfast on the _____. Check it out: John 21:4-14.
Bible Situation - New Testament #11 The first Christians lived together and shared everything they owned or earned. They gave food to _____. Check it out: Acts 2:43-47.	**Bible Situation - New Testament #12** Special servants called _____ were chosen by the first Christians to make sure the widows were not neglected in the distribution of food. Check it out: Acts 6:1-7.
Bible Situation - New Testament #13 _____ gave Paul, Timothy, and Silas a place to stay and fed them so that they could work for God in the area where she lived. Check it out: Acts 16:11-15.	**Bible Situation - New Testament #14** The book of James says _____ without _____ is dead. Believing in God, but not feeding those who are hungry is wrong. Wishing hungry people peace is not enough. Check it out: James 2:14-17.

Contemporary Situation Game Cards (1/3)

Contemporary Situation #1

Althof was just elected to student council. The council wants to help the students to do something to make a difference for hungry people. How can they set an example?

Contemporary Situation #2

Asa's church collected money at Vacation Bible School to help feed hungry people. How can they use it to help set an example?

Contemporary Situation #3

Benjamin sees a lot of kids wasting food everyday at lunch. What could he do to make a difference and to set an example?

Contemporary Situation #4

Brianna's elderly neighbor has a hard time getting to the store. Brianna's mother says the woman does not eat well and also does not have much money. What example could Brianna set?

Contemporary Situation #5

Bryant lives on a farm. This year his family garden produced more than his family could eat or preserve. What example could Bryant set for others?

Contemporary Situation #6

Byoung noticed recently that another boy in his class often has little or no food for lunch. The boy tries not to let anyone see. How can Byoung set an example?

Contemporary Situation #7

Connie saw a show about starving children on television and it gave her nightmares. Now every time she sees an advertisement she changes the channel or flips the page of the magazine. What could she do to set an example?

Contemporary Situation #8

Denelza's pastor announced that the Sunday School will be collecting food for the church's food pantry. How can she help and set an example?

Contemporary Situation Game Cards (2/3)

Contemporary Situation #9	Contemporary Situation #10
Djemillah's priest preached a sermon on hunger. He ended by saying everyone can do something about hunger. He asked each person to choose something to do and to write it on a piece of paper to put in the offering plate next week. What could Djemillah do to set an example?	Emillio's mother just had surgery and his father is very busy taking care of his family and his job. How could Emillio set an example?
Contemporary Situation #11	**Contemporary Situation #12**
Georgia feels like she hears about hungry people or programs to help hungry people every day. She feels guilty that she has food and others don't. There are so many things that need to be done that she can't figure out what to do. How can Georgia set an example?	Abdul saw on the news that people were starving in a country half way around the world. It made him very sad, but he doesn't know what he can do to help. How could he set an example?
Contemporary Situation #13	**Contemporary Situation #14**
Jennifer goes to a church that doesn't do anything to feed hungry people. It bothers her a lot. What can she do to set an example?	Lisa's church had a special dinner. Too much food was prepared and now there is a lot left over. What could Lisa do to set an example and to avoid waste?
Contemporary Situation #15	**Contemporary Situation #16**
Lo Duc's Boy Scout troop gave him grocery bags to distribute for Scouting for Food. People are supposed to fill them and place them in front of their houses for pick-up. The food will go to a food pantry to help hungry people. How can Lo Duc set an example and help make the program a success?	Mark heard about a group that helps to glean the fields after the farmers are done harvesting. The food they collect is given to several food programs. How could Mark set an example?

Contemporary Situation Game Cards (3/3)

Contemporary Situation #17

Michael noticed that the food for the food pantry often piles up and sits there for weeks. What could Michael do to help set an example?

Contemporary Situation #18

Nikki's youth club was asked to change one eating habit that would make a small difference in combating hunger. What could Nikki do to set an example?

Contemporary Situation #19

Rebecca heard about a program called Project Heifer. They send live animals to countries all around the world to help people learn how to produce their own food. How can Rebecca set an example?

Contemporary Situation #20

Rita's youth group has been studying hunger around the world. What can they do to set an example and to make a difference for hungry people around the globe?

Contemporary Situation #21

Tanya's church has a homeless shelter. They need food to serve their guests and money to buy other food supplies. What can her youth group do to set an example?

Contemporary Situation #22

Thomas has always wanted to volunteer in a soup kitchen. What could he do to follow through on his idea and to set an example?

Contemporary Situation #23

Tirena's church was told they could use the empty lot next door in any way they want. How could it be used to set an example?

Contemporary Situation #24

Naomi recently learned that people who have no food occasionally knock on the pastor's door and ask for help. How could Naomi set an example?

Recognizing the Hungry

Isaiah 58:10

If you offer your food to the hungry and satisfy the needs of the afflicted, then your light shall rise in the darkness and your gloom be like the noonday.

Learn

Participants will express the message of Matthew 25:35-45 by adding movement to interpret the song "When I Was Hungry."

Locate

► Bible
► Copy machine or printer
► Costume pieces or hats (optional)
► Instruments for musical accompaniment (optional)
► Paper for copy machine or printer
► Resource sheet: "'When I Was Hungry' Music" (below)
► Resource sheet: "'When I Was Hungry' Movements" (below)

Advance Preparation

► Duplicate copies of the music and the movement resource sheets for the participants.
► If costumes will be used, assemble bib overalls, t-shirts, and caps for those who portray the "have-nots" and suit coats and fancy hats for those who portray the "haves."

Lead

From ancient churches through current congregations, dance, gesture. and movement have been incorporated into worship, education, and outreach to convey themes related to hunger. Dance is used in conjunction with songs, readings, and prayers in services of worship. In education events, it helps learners explore and experience concepts related to providing food for those in need. Fortunately, these art forms are available to everyone regardless of ability and age. Inexperienced and trained dancers can share in creating pieces that range from simple to elaborate and from concrete to abstract. In this lesson, participants will combine movement with the message of the song "When I Was Hungry" and present it in various settings to raise awareness and to prompt action related to hunger causes and concerns. In the process they will be helped to recognize the hungry who are all around them. They will also be assured of Jesus' blessing for those who recognize his face in the faces of those in need.

Explain that the class will listen to, and possibly learn, a song titled "When I Was Hungry." In addition, they will add movement to convey the theme. The music emphasizes the message of Matthew 25:35-45—when we minister to those in need we show love to Jesus through our actions. Play or sing the song for the group. Then take time to read and study the words of the verses before preparing the dance interpretations that illustrate each stanza.

Begin the project by organizing the participants into two groups, labeled "haves" and "have-nots." If costumes are used, distribute bib overalls, t-shirts, and caps to the "have-nots" to identify them with the poor. Give the "haves" formal attire like suit coats and business or fancy hats to connect them with the rich.

Distribute copies of the movement resource sheet and review the procedure for the project. As a group, listen to or read the words of the first verse. Then review and practice the suggested movements. For the remaining six verses, the entire class can do them together or small groups may prepare and portray each of them.

When the class is ready to present their parts, ask the two groups to move to separate sides of the room. This can help highlight the physical and cultural distance between the "haves" and the "have-nots." As the song is sung each verse is enacted with the movements.

During the preparation time and following the presentation of "When I Was Hungry," be sure to process the message and the meaning of the words and movements with the participants. Help the group realize that there are hungry and hurting people all around them. As an additional activity, use a positive approach to interpreting the Bible passage and the verses of the song. Although the scripture talks about those who turned away and did not see, it also commends those who did respond to the needs of others. Re-read the scripture passages, Isaiah 58:10 and Matthew 25:35-45, and use music and movement to show how this situation could have turned out differently. Re-write each verse, such as:

When I was hungry
you gave me something to eat.

When I was naked
you found shoes for my feet.

When I was thirsty
you gave me some of your wine.

I needed your hand, and you
shared your time.

Choose movements to interpret the message in a positive manner and present the activity again. Remind the participants that they will both be blessed and be a blessing through helping others in Jesus' name.

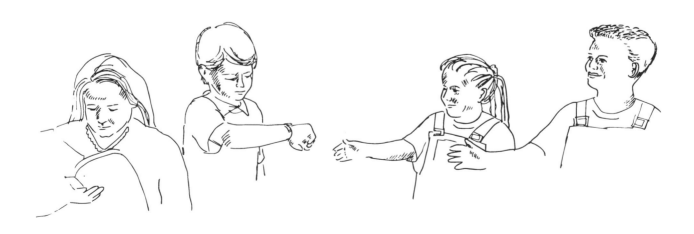

"When I Was Hungry" Music

Words and music
by Joe Dowell

1. When I was hun-gry You gave me nothing to eat
2. We saw the hun-gry. We saw the naked too.
3. But when your bro-thers Cry out for help from you

When I was na-ked No coat or shoes for my feet.
We saw the thirst-y But, Lord, we didn't see you.
And you turn your backs, I feel the sorrow too.

When I was thirst-y You gave me none of your wine.
'Cause if we had, Lord, We would have given you wine.
When your ears are deaf To your brother's plea.

I needed your hand, and you Didn't have time.
We'd have offered a hand; Yes, we would have had time.
Your heart is hard, and you Can't hear me.

CODA

2. We saw the

How I needed your hand and you didn't have time.

4. When I was hungry
   You gave me none of your bread.
   When I was weary
   You had no place for my head.
   When I was crying
   You didn't comfort me
   You just left me to my misery.

5. We saw the hungry;
   We saw the weary too.
   We heard them crying,
   But, Lord, we didn't hear you.
   'Cause if we had, Lord,
   We would have run to your side.
   A call from the Master
   Would not be denied.

6. But when your brothers
   Cry out for help from you,
   And you turn your backs
   I feel the sorrow too.
   When your ears are deaf
   To your brother's plea,
   Your heart is hard,
   And you can't hear me.

7. When I was hungry
   You gave me nothing to eat
   When I was naked,
   No coat or shoes for my feet.
   You gave me none of your wine.
   I needed your hand,
   And you didn't have time.

CODA
How I needed your hand.
And you didn't have time.

"When I Was Hungry" Movements

	Lyrics	Movements
1	When I was hungry you gave me nothing to eat. When I was naked no coat or shoes for my feet. When I was thirsty you gave me none of your wine. I needed your hand, and you didn't have time.	Through writhing and twisting motions the "have-nots" show the intense suffering of hunger and thirst. Clenched fists are brought to the center of the body and turned one against the other. Movements to shield and conceal the body show the indignity of nakedness. Simultaneously the "haves" mingle with each other, oblivious to the human suffering near them. At the end of the verse, each "have-not" reaches out, hands open to the "haves" who busy themselves as if checking their phones or their watches.
2	We saw the hungry. We saw the naked too. We saw the thirsty but, Lord, we didn't see you. 'Cause if we had, Lord, we would have given you wine. We'd have offered a hand; Yes, we would have had time.	The "have-nots" repeat their previous movement but remain fixed in one spot. The "haves" stroll through the group, taking casual notice but remaining unimpressed by what they see and not recognizing Jesus in anyone. Toward the end of the verse, the "have-nots" form a tight circle with their backs to one another as the "haves" return to their original position.
3	But when your brothers cry out for help from you, and you turn your backs, I feel the sorrow, too. When your ears are deaf to your brother's plea, your heart is hard, and you can't hear me.	The "have-nots" join hands and rhythmically raise their heads and torsos in a wailing motion. The "haves" line up with their backs to the "have-nots," arms linked, and appear interested only in each other. The "have-nots" end the verse with heads bowed, arms limp at their sides, weary of begging.
4	When I was hungry you gave me none of your bread. When I was weary you had no place for my head. When I was crying you didn't comfort me. You just left me to my misery.	The "haves" turn around to face the "have-nots," but stay in their line, almost shoulder to shoulder but no longer connected. One person from the "have-nots" rises and approaches the first "have," placing cupped hands in the hands of the "haves." This movement symbolizes hunger. The first "have-not" promptly is pushed away and reels around to face the next "have" with the same results. Each "have" is confronted individually with the hand gesture but turns it away. As the "have-not" leaves the last "have" and twirls to a place in front of and a few feet away from him or her, the "have-not" stops and assumes the hunger pose. A second "have-not" rises and approaches the aligned "haves." This time the gesture of confrontation represents weariness. The "have-not" attempts to rest his or her head on the shoulder of the "have" but is shrugged off by each in turn. Ultimately the second "have-not" lands with head on the shoulder of the first "have-not." The "have-not" then assumes the weariness pose. ▶

Lyrics	Movements
	A third "have-not" then rises and approaches the "haves." The "have-not" holds his or her face as if crying and seeks comfort from each "have." The "have-not" is pushed away in the same manner as the others. The "have-not" ends up leaning against the first and second "have-nots" in the crying pose. They then, as one body, shuffle slowly a few feet further away from the "haves'" line.
5 We saw the hungry; We saw the weary too. We heard them crying, but, Lord, we didn't hear you. 'Cause if we had, Lord, we would have run to your side. A call from the Master would not be denied.	A fourth "have-not" rises as the verse begins and approaches the first "have" with the hunger gesture, the next with the weariness gesture, and the last with the crying gesture. The "have-not" is brushed aside as the others were. As the "have-not" leaves the line, he or she stops momentarily between the "haves" and the huddled "have-nots." Then while the lyric "we would have run to your side" is sung, the "haves" move in unison with arms outstretched to touch the solitary "have-not" as if they all suddenly realized that this last person was Jesus. Just as they reach the fourth "have-not," she or he moves away from them to join the other "have-nots."
6 But when your brothers cry out for help from you, and you turn your backs I feel the sorrow too. When your ears are deaf to your brother's plea, your heart is hard, and you can't hear me.	The supplication theme of verse three is repeated. This time the "have-nots" stand in a cluster facing the audience with their backs to the "haves." They lift their arms and heads upward slowly, only to drop back down, bodies bent to the floor. The "haves" remain in their places searching, looking past the "have-nots" for the vanished Christ. The "have-nots" rise again, and turn to face the "haves." At that moment, the "haves" sharply turn around, link arms, and walk away slowly. They end up in their original position mingling one with another. The "have-nots" also move back to their original position.
7 When I was hungry you gave me nothing to eat. When I was naked, no coat or shoes for my feet. When I was thirsty you gave me none of your wine. I needed your hand, and you didn't have time. CODA How I needed your hand and you didn't have time.	The dance for this verse is exactly like verse one. The "have-nots" hold their ending position, reaching to the "haves" with open hands. The "haves" stroll casually off the stage, having left everything just as it was.

Movements: Cornerstone Community of Stanton, VA – *Liturgical Dance.*

Music: Washington, DC: Bread for the World. Used by permission.

Caring through Prayer

<u>John 21:17b</u>
And he said to him, 'Lord, you know everything; you know that I love you.' Jesus said to him, 'Feed my sheep.'

Learn

Participants will retell the story of Jesus and Peter, consider people who are emotionally and spiritually hungry, and participate in a prayer activity to remember them.

Locate

▶ Basket
▶ Bible
▶ Copy machine or printer
▶ Crayons
▶ Markers
▶ Paper for copy machine or printer
▶ Pencils
▶ Resource sheet: "Pattern for Bread and Person"
▶ Scissors

Advance Preparation

Duplicate and cut out the bread pattern and the figure pattern for each participant. Separate the cut outs into two piles.

Lead

Peter wanted to serve Jesus. When the two met on the shore after Jesus' resurrection, Jesus instructed Peter: "Feed my lambs. Tend my sheep." This story is a reminder that there are people like Peter who are emotionally and spiritually, rather than physically, hungry. Many hurting, lonely people who hunger for love and affection need to be fed by people who care for them. Through this activity the participants will identify some of these people's needs and respond to them with prayer.

Welcome the participants to the session. Arrange chairs in a circle or sit with the group on the floor. Ask each person to share one interesting thing that has happened since the last meeting. Show concern for and interest in the responses which are offered.

After a time of casual conversation, read the Bible story for the lesson, John 21:4-18. Assign four people the following parts:

▶ Narrator
▶ Jesus
▶ "The disciple whom Jesus loved"
▶ Peter.

Offer background information on the passage before reading it. This story is set after Jesus' death and resurrection. Since fishing was the job most of the disciples gave up to become Jesus' helpers, once Jesus had left them, they returned to their previous occupation. Peter is the central character of this episode. In previous chapters of John, it was reported that Peter denied knowing

Jesus three times. The appearance, recorded in John 21, is described as the third time that Jesus revealed himself to his disciples after the resurrection.

Invite the participants to read their assigned parts of the scripture passage. Following the reading, have the learners imagine more of what took place in the story. Ask questions like:

► How might the disciples have felt about Jesus' suggestion concerning fishing?

► What must the disciples have thought about Jesus' advice after they caught so many fish?

► What would it be like to share a meal with Jesus?

► How do you think Peter felt when he saw Jesus again?

► Why do you think Jesus asked Peter the same question three times?

► What do you think Jesus meant when he told Peter to feed his sheep?

Provide a summary to conclude this portion of the lesson. This story begins with Jesus helping the disciples to catch fish. Then Jesus lovingly feeds them a meal on the shore. Finally, Jesus shows Peter that he still loves him and gives Peter a job to do. Jesus called himself the Good Shepherd. He took care of people just like a shepherd cares for a flock of sheep. When Jesus was preparing to return to heaven he asked Peter to take care of and to feed his sheep. Matthew 25 makes it clear that it is the job of every Christian to feed Jesus' sheep just as if they were caring for Christ himself.

It is very important to share food with those who have a physical hunger. But, Peter had a different kind of hunger. He was hungry for Jesus' love and acceptance. Peter needed to be forgiven by Jesus. Jesus knew what Peter needed and was willing to feed Peter.

There are many people who feel like Peter. They are hungry emotionally and spiritually rather than physically. Some of them might be abused, angry, guilty, hurt, lonely, rejected, sad, scared, or unloved. Distribute the people figures, as well as markers or pens, and have the participants write these words on a cutout. Allow the group to suggest other words to describe spiritual hunger and add them to the figures as well. After the cutouts are prepared, invite the group to trade figures so each person has one for the next part of the activity.

Distribute the cutouts of the loaves of bread. Discuss what solutions are needed to feed the hungers listed on the people figures. For example, someone who is lonely needs a friend to listen to him or her. An individual who is guilty requires forgiveness. These solutions should be written on the bread loaf cutouts. When each need or hunger has been discussed and a solution has been suggested and recorded on a shape, the cutouts can be placed in a bread basket and set in the middle of the group.

When the basket is full, pass it around the circle and ask each person to take one piece of bread. Note that the cutout does not need to be the one the person made. While holding the bread, the person is to pray for one way of feeding the hungry. Allow a time of silence after each person's prayer. Continue around the circle until everyone has addressed one hunger with a solution.

After this prayer activity, encourage the participants to take the pieces of bread and the figures of people home with them to continue to pray for those who hunger in the ways described on the cutouts. Remind the learners that they may be the answer to one of the prayers. Challenge them to put their prayers into action in helping to feed Jesus' sheep.

Pattern for Bread and Person

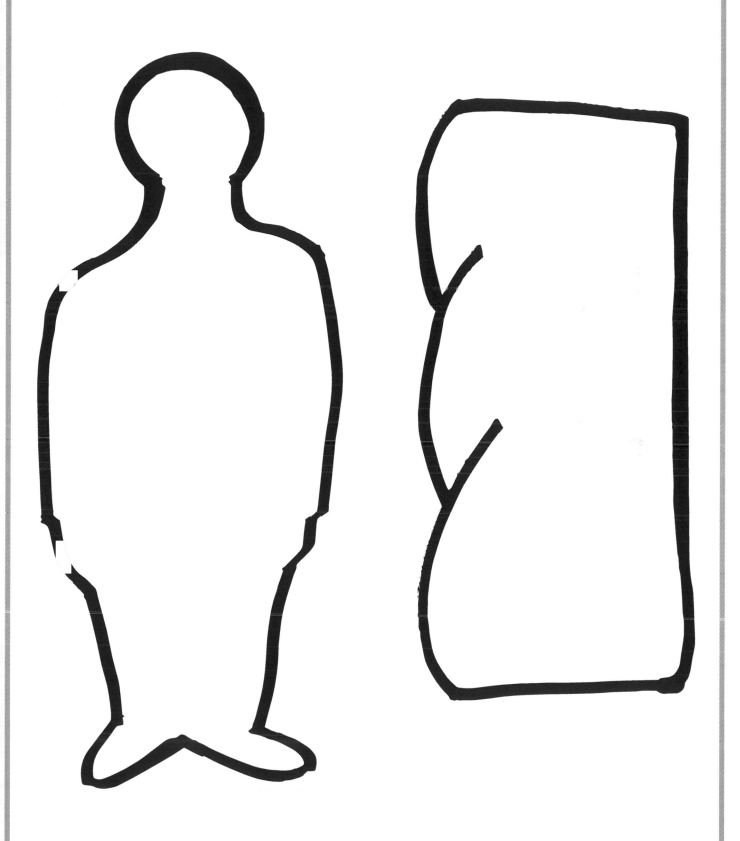

Sharing Your Resources

<u>John 15:13</u>

**No one has greater love than this,
to lay down one's life for one's friends.**

Learn

Participants will consider the theme of sacrificial giving by making paper bag body puppets and sharing the Japanese folktale "The Rabbit In the Moon."

Locate

- Bags, brown paper grocery type
- Bags, plastic
- Bible
- Chairs, 2
- Copy machine or printer
- Glue
- Markers
- Paper, construction
- Paper for copy machine or printer
- Props, artificial or real
  - Apple
  - Banana
  - Grapes
  - Orange
  - Pear
  - Seaweed
  - Sticks
- Resource sheet: "'The Rabbit in the Moon' Script"
- Rubber bands, medium – 2 per puppet
- Scissors
- Staplers
- Staples
- Yarn

Advance Preparation

- Duplicate copies of "'The Rabbit in the Moon' Script."
- Set up two chairs to be used during the puppet show.
- Scatter the props around the room for the characters to pick up during the presentation.

Lead

A Japanese folktale, "The Rabbit In the Moon" (Pratt, David and Elsa Kula. *Magic Animals of Japan.* Berkeley, CA: Parnassus Press, 1967), emphasizes the message of John 15:3, "laying down one's life for a friend." By engaging in a dramatic re-enactment of the story the participants will discover that each person can use his or her own unique gifts to help those who are hungry. In this lesson, the class will create paper grocery bag body puppets to represent the characters in the book and use them to share this message with others.

Introduce the theme of "giving for others" to the class by sharing a summary of the story:

"The Rabbit In The Moon" is a Japanese folktale of an old man who lives in the moon. One day he decides to go to earth to locate the kindest animal in the forest. Disguised as a beggar, the man asks a variety of animals for food. Each animal brings the man something to eat. Although the rabbit too searches for food to share, he is sad because he does not find anything to present to the man. So, instead of food, he offers the man sticks, and tells him to use them to build a bonfire. Rabbit meat, he says, is very delicious. The old man realizes that because the rabbit is willing to offer the gift of himself, he is the kindest animal in the forest.

Explain that the learners will make puppets and use them to present this folktale. Invite each person to choose one of the following characters to construct for the skit:

► Bear

► Duck

► Lamb

► Lion

► Monkey

► Old man

► Rabbit

► Wolf

Depending on the number of participants, additional animals may be incorporated into the script or several students may construct the same type of character.

Demonstrate the procedure for making the puppets. Explain that the group is going to recycle brown paper grocery bags and plastic food or garbage sacks into body puppets. This type of puppet is worn, rather than held, to operate it.

Start with a full size brown paper grocery bag. The bottom flap becomes the puppet's head and the rest of the bag forms the body. Pick a full sheet of construction paper and glue it to the body portion of the bag. Cut another piece of construction paper to fit the flap and glue it in place as well. Decorate the head and the body of the character with markers and construction paper pieces.

Make a neck strap by cutting a 30" by 2" piece of yarn. Staple the center of the yarn to the middle of the top of the bag. For arms, cut two 18" x 2" strips of plastic bag. Tie a rubber band to the end of each piece of plastic. Staple the other end of each arm strip to the paper bag, just below the flap.

Provide the materials and allow time for the participants to create their puppets. Offer individualized instruction and encouragement during the process.

Once the puppets are completed, invite each person to wear and work his or her animal or person. Tell them to tie the yarn around their neck and to slip the rubber bands over their wrists. The person's motions and movements manipulate the puppet.

Gather the group in a circle on the floor or on chairs. Explain that the story will be presented in a participatory manner. One person, serving as the narrator, will guide the telling of the folktale. This person should read the lines slowly, giving the puppeteers ample time to act out their parts. When the narrator mentions a particular animal, that serves as a signal for the puppeteer wearing that character to get ready to participate in the story. Give the narrator a copy of the script. If desired, give each actor a copy of the narration as well or have a leader whisper words to each participant, in turn, having the person repeat the words loudly as if the puppet were saying the lines. Tell the group that the props mentioned in the script have been scattered around the area, and that they are to look for and to locate them at the appropriate point in the play. The following props go with each character:

► Apple - Lamb

► Banana - Monkey

► Grapes - Wolf

► Orange - Lion

- ▶ Pear - Bear
- ▶ Seaweed - Duck
- ▶ Sticks - Rabbit

Once the instructions are shared, invite everyone to get ready to begin the action. Present the play and tell the story.

At the conclusion of the puppet show, invite the participants to share their reactions to the story. Ask questions like: How were all of the animals generous? Since every animal helped the old man, why was the rabbit considered the kindest of all? Most people will answer because the rabbit was willing to give of herself. Emphasize that the willingness of the rabbit to give its life for the old man does not imply that the children should copy the rabbit but rather they should identify ways that they can give of

themselves for others, especially for hungry people.

Ask the group to brainstorm some ways to be like the rabbit, giving of themselves for someone else, especially for those in need of food. Consider responses such as sharing creativity, energy, ideas, money, talents, and time. If desired, develop each suggestion into a specific action plan including the students' involvement in their families, congregations, schools, and communities.

Conclude by considering ways in which Christians are called to be like the "rabbit" because of the example Jesus set through his life, death, and resurrection. Invite each person to make a commitment to do one "rabbit-like" thing in the coming week. Conclude the session, if appropriate, by offering these reflections as silent or shared prayers.

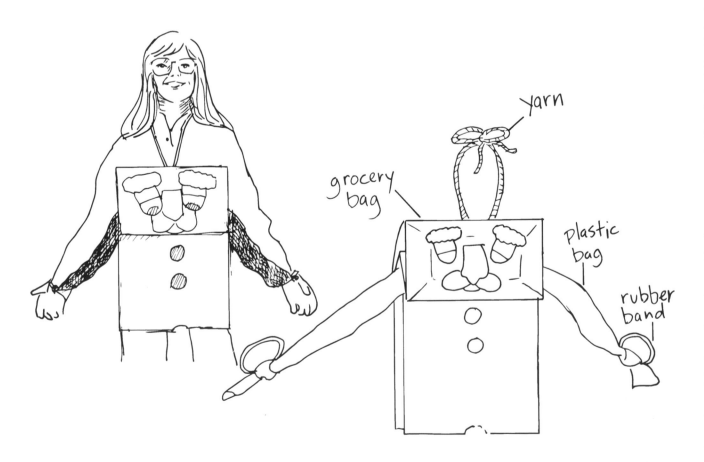

"The Rabbit in the Moon" Script

[The old man stands on a chair. Each animal bows, steps forward, or reacts as its name is called.]

Narrator: Our story begins with an old man who lives in the moon. As he looked down on the earth he saw many interesting animals in the forest. He saw a monkey, a wolf, a bear, and a lion. Near the stream in the meadow at the edge of the forest he saw a lamb, a duck, and a rabbit.

The old man said:

Old Man: I wonder which animal is the kindest animal in the world.

[Jumps off chair and stands in the circle.]

Narrator: The old man jumped down out of the moon, turned himself into a beggar, and walked into the forest.

The old man said:

Old Man: I'm hungry. I'm so hungry.

Narrator: When all the animals heard the old man, they said together:

Animals: *[Animals talk to each other.]*

Let's help the old man.

Narrator: They talked among themselves and decided to go out and look for some good things to eat.

Animals: *[All the animals go to look for food. Each finds an item to give to the old man.]*

Narrator: The old man waited patiently until all the animals returned.

Then the monkey said:

Monkey: *[Monkey walks to the man and offers him the banana.]*

Konnichi Wa. (Good Afternoon.) I found you something delicious to eat. I found you a banana.

Old Man: *[Man takes the banana.]*

Arigato. (Thank you.) I like bananas.

Narrator: And the monkey was very pleased to be able to help the old man.

[Monkey returns to place.]

Next the wolf came to the old man and said:

Wolf: *[Wolf walks to the man and offers him the grapes.]*

Konnichi Wa. I found something good for you to eat. I love grapes. These are for you.

Old Man: *[Man takes the grapes.]*

Arigato. Grapes are very good. I will enjoy them.

Narrator: The wolf was very glad that he could help the old man.

[Wolf returns to place.]

The bear came to the old man next. He said:

Bear: *[Bear walks to the man and offers him the pear.]*

Konnichi Wa. I found you something to eat. Pears are very good. Now you will not be hungry.

Old Man: *[Man takes the pear.]*

Arigato. You are very kind.

Narrator: It made the bear happy to help the old man.

[Bear returns to place.]

The lion, too, had found something for the old man to eat.

Lion: *[Lion walks to man and offers him the orange.]*

Konnichi Wa. I found you something to eat. This orange will be good for you.

Old Man: *[Man takes the orange.]*

Arigato. I love fresh oranges.

Narrator: That made the lion very happy.

[Lion returns to place.]

The meadow animals had also looked for food. The lamb came to the old man.

Lamb: *[Lamb walks to man and offers him the apple.]*

Konnichi Wa. I like to eat apples. I found one to share with you so you will not be hungry.

Old Man: *[Man takes the apple.]*

Arigato. I will like it.

Narrator: The lamb bounced off happily.

[Lamb returns to place.]

The duck waddled to see the old man.

Duck *[Duck walks to man and offers seaweed.]*

I went to my stream and found you this nice fresh seaweed. It is full of vitamins.

Old Man: *[Man takes seaweed.]*

Arigato. Vitamins will help me.

Narrator: The duck let out a happy quack and returned to the meadow stream.

[Duck returns to place.]

Then it was the rabbit's turn.

[Rabbit walks to man.]

She came up to the old man crying. The old man said:

Old Man: What is the matter?

Narrator: But the rabbit kept crying. The old man said:

Old Man: Don't cry rabbit. What is wrong?

Rabbit: I couldn't find you anything to eat. I feel so sad.

Old Man: That's okay. The other animals brought me many things to eat. I will not be hungry.

Rabbit: *[Rabbit offers man sticks.]*

Old man. I brought some sticks. If you build a big bonfire, rabbit meat is very delicious.

Old Man: *[Man takes sticks.]*

You, rabbit, are very kind. You mean you'd be willing to give your life to help me?

Rabbit: I would if you really needed it.

Old Man: You, rabbit, are the kindest animal in the whole world. Come with me back to the moon.

[Man and rabbit stand on chairs.]

Narrator: In Japan, and in other countries around the world, if you look at the full moon, you don't see the picture of a man, but instead you might see the face of a rabbit.

Multiplying the Food

John 6:9

"There is a boy here who has five barley loaves and two fish. But what are they among so many people?"

Learn

Participants will review the story of Jesus feeding the multitude by retelling it in the form of a rhythm story.

Locate

► Bible

► Copy machine or printer

► Paper for copy machine or printer

► Resource sheet: "Multiplying the Food Rhythm Story"

Advance Preparation

► Duplicate a copy of the rhythm story resource sheet for each participant.

Lead

Although the New Testament story of the feeding of the 5,000 is a familiar narrative, there is always something new to be learned from it. An important message—then and now—is that with God's power, every effort made to feed the hungry will be multiplied. When Jesus' followers work together, a little can turn into a lot with God's help. In this lesson the participants will use a rhythm story as a fun way of learning this important truth.

Introduce the theme of the lesson by reading the story from John 6:1-14. Then, invite the group to share the account in a participatory manner called a rhythm story. Distribute a copy of the resource sheet to each participant. Choose five leaders or organize the participants into five small groups to chant assigned verses. Teach the refrain to the entire class and invite everyone to repeat it at the appropriate times. To use this narrative as an echo story, have the leader or small group for each verse chant a line and invite the rest of the participants to repeat or echo it back. When using the echo technique, begin by establishing a clapping rhythm to accompany the lines. A slap on the knees and a clap of the hands works well. Involve the students in the story, and conclude by sharing ways in which they can work to feed the hungry, individually and collectively.

One way to expand this activity would be to have the students write additional verses to the rhythm story. Together brainstorm a list of things the class members could do to share food with hungry people. Individually or in small groups, choose one idea from the list to develop. Instruct the participants to write a four line verse, in the same style as the chant, about their way of sharing food. As a whole group, recite the additional verses and follow each with the refrain.

Multiplying the Food Rhythm Story

Person or Group One: People came to hear Jesus from all around.
They came from the country; they came from the town.
They were hungry to hear what Jesus would say,
and crowded to be near him in every way.

All: You can do it, you just have to try,
and God will give the power to multiply.

Person or Group Two: People listened all day at Jesus' feet.
It grew late and the folks had nothing to eat.
To send them off hungry just wouldn't be kind,
Jesus told the disciples to see what food they could find.

All: You can do it, you just have to try,
and God will give the power to multiply.

Person or Group Three: As they searched, they discovered one little boy.
His five loaves and two fishes, he gave with joy.
It surely was a very generous deed.
But it wouldn't be all the food they would need.

All: You can do it, you just have to try,
and God will give the power to multiply.

Person or Group Four: Jesus blessed it, and broke it, and passed it about.
The disciples thought that he would surely run out.
Everyone there had much more than their fill,
and believe it or not, there were leftovers still!

All: You can do it, you just have to try,
and God will give the power to multiply.

Person or Group Five: You may think that there is little you can do,
but God will multiply your gifts and talents, too.
You can help feed hungry people everywhere.
and with God's help, you can show that you care.

All: You can do it, you just have to try,
and God will give the power to multiply.

Remembering the Hungry

Matthew 6:11

Give us this day our daily bread.

Learn

Participants will thank God for their daily bread and create wooden spoon reminders to help meet the needs of the hungry.

Locate

- Bible
- Brushes, paint
- Containers for paint
- Covering for work surface
- Eye screws
- Flowers, dried or silk (optional)
- Markers
- Paint, acrylic
- Paint marker, thin white
- Poster board
- Sample wooden spoon craft
- Scissors
- Shirts or smocks to protect clothing from paint
- Spoons, wooden – 1 per person
- Raffia or thin satin ribbon

Advance Preparation

- For young children, position the eye screws into the ends of the spoons ahead of time.
- Prepare a sample of the wooden spoon project for use in the game.
- Use markers to prepare a poster board sign which reads, "I was hungry and you fed me."

Lead

In the Lord's Prayer, we use the words that Jesus taught his followers—then and now—to petition God for the gift of daily bread. Unfortunately, in a society where food is plentiful for the majority, it is easy to forget about those who do not receive an adequate share of something as common as bread, let alone the requirements for a healthy diet. Jesus told of the importance of caring for those in need of food in the parable of the last judgment when he said: "I was hungry and you fed me." In this lesson, the participants will create a wooden spoon to hang in the eating area of their homes. The artwork will help them remember the hungry and be more aware of their own eating choices.

Explain to the participants that many people do not have the bread, or daily food, which they need in order to survive. It is important that those who do have ample food remember to pray daily for those who do not. Tell the group that they will be making a decorative spoon which will be a reminder to pray for, and to act on behalf of, the hungry.

Gather around a covered work surface. If the group is young, provide old shirts or smocks to protect clothing from paint spills. Distribute a wooden spoon to each artist and make the group aware of the containers of paints and the brushes in each of them that are available for their use. Instruct the participants to choose a color of paint for their spoon which will look attractive when hung in the eating areas of their homes. Encourage the painters to apply a light coat of paint on the spoons or else they will take a long time to dry. When the spoons are painted, set them aside to dry.

While the painted spoons are drying, have the participants meet in a circle on the floor. Use a sample spoon craft as a prop for a game. Begin the game by saying, "This spoon reminds me to pray for the homeless people who eat at the local soup kitchen." Then pass the spoon to the player on the right. That person repeats the phrase, "This spoon reminds me ..." and finishes the sentence with an idea of his or her own. Encourage the students to be as creative as possible in their responses. Also ask them to be specific in their suggestions; to pray for a particular group or individual in need, rather than simply for all hungry people.

Some examples are:

► ... to be thankful for the food I have.

► ... to bring food to donate to church next Sunday.

► ... to eat things that are good for me.

► ... to not waste the food I am blessed to have.

► ... to volunteer at the food bank.

Continue the game for as long as the participants have new contributions to make.

When the painted spoons are dry, move them to a table where decorating supplies are available. Direct the students to make a simple bow from paper raffia or satin ribbon and to tie it to the spoon handle. If dried or silk flowers are available, tie them to the spoon handle as well.

If this step wasn't completed prior to the class, provide eye screws for the crafters. Show them how to screw them into the ends of the spoons to allow the completed project to be easily hung in their eating area at home.

Use a white paint marker to write the words, "I was hungry and you fed me," on the bowl of the spoon. Display the poster with these words so that they can be easily copied. Some participants could work on this step while others are decorating, so that less paint markers will be needed.

When all steps have been completed, meet again in a circle with each participant holding his or her spoon. Close the session in prayer, asking God to help remind each person to care about, to pray for, and to help the hungry whenever possible.

Spreading the Word

Luke 16:20-21

And at his gate lay a poor man named Lazarus, covered with sores, who longed to satisfy his hunger with what fell from the rich man's table.

Learn

Participants will explore the issue of world hunger through an activity involving a smorgasbord of breads from different continents.

Locate

- ▶ Bible
- ▶ Bread, various types such as chapitas, corn, marbled, rice cakes, rye, tortillas, and wheat
- ▶ Bread, uncut loaf
- ▶ Chalk or markers
- ▶ Chalkboard or newsprint
- ▶ Copy machine or printer
- ▶ Knife
- ▶ Map of the world
- ▶ Napkins
- ▶ Paper – brown, tan, white
- ▶ Paper for copy machine or printer
- ▶ Pencils or pens
- ▶ Resource sheet: "Sharing Food in a Hungry World Litany"
- ▶ Scissors

Advance Preparation

- ▶ Cut brown, tan, and white paper into the shape and size of a slice of bread, one piece per person.
- ▶ Duplicate copies of the Sharing Food in a Hungry World Litany for the participants.

Lead

In the story of Lazarus and the uncaring rich man, Luke 16:19-31, a hungry beggar is turned away without being helped. Although the wealthy man felt satisfied, he did not share his bounty or tend to the needs of someone less fortunate. It is sometimes easy for people who have food to forget about those who struggle to meet their daily needs. While some people enjoy plenty, others exist on the brink of starvation. In this lesson, the large scale problem of world hunger will be explored through a smorgasbord of breads from different continents.

As an introduction to the lesson, ask the participants to name a type of food which is part of almost every meal. Bread, in various forms and flavors, is sometimes served three times a day. It may take the form of toast for breakfast, sandwiches for lunch, and rolls for dinner. Tell the young people that for many people of the world bread is the mainstay of their diet. For some, it may be all they eat in a day. Acquaint the pupils with various types of bread which are commonly used on the seven continents of the world. These may include:

- Africa - chapitas
- Antarctica - marbled
- Asia - rice cakes
- Australia - wheat
- Europe - rye
- North America - cornbread
- South and Central America - tortillas.

Invite the group to sample several selections.

Show the participants a world map and tell them that they will be learning more about the distribution of people and food in the global setting. On the world map, point out the five most populated continents: Africa, Asia, Europe, North America, and South America. Note that Australia has a very small percentage, 0.5, of the population of the world. Provide information on the percentage of the world's population of more than 7 billion people living on each major continent. Write these facts on a chalkboard or a piece of newsprint (they are rounded so they don't exactly add up to 100%):

- Africa - 17%
- Asia - 60%
- Europe - 10%
- North America - 7%
- South America - 6%
- Australia - 0.5%

Divide the participants into six groups representing the main continents. Approximate the percentages as closely as possible. For example, in a group of twenty-five participants, the Asia group might have fifteen members, Africa four or five, Europe two, South America two, and North America one.

Hold up an uncut loaf of bread and explain that it represents all the food that is eaten in the world in one day. State that, for many reasons, nearly one billion people on the continents experience severe hunger. In fact, the places with the most people have the least amount of food. Share the number of undernourished people in the world with the group by reading the following data compiled from the Food and Agriculture Organization of the United Nations and UNICEF:

- Africa - 20%
- Asia - 11%
- South America - 6%
- Australia/Oceania - 6%
- North America/Europe - 2%

Distribute the Sharing Food In a Hungry World litany. Choose a leader and have the participants read it together, with each continent group responding in turn.

At the conclusion of the litany, divide the uncut loaf of bread among the number of people in the group. Tell the learners that our goal should be an equal, and just, amount of food for everyone in the world.

Continue the activity by talking with the learners about ways in which bread is used in their own lives. Brainstorm how this taken for granted staple may be used more sparingly. These ideas may range from buying it at a surplus store, finding out what grocery stores and bakeries do with day old bread, or using stale bread for crumbs or croutons rather than throwing it away.

Pass out the papers which have been cut into the shapes of bread slices. Provide markers or pens and ask each learner to draw or write a way in which he or she will commit to using bread more carefully and creatively so that all people of the world may have more to eat.

Sharing Food In a Hungry World

Leader: The earth is the Lord's. The Lord created the world and all who dwell therein.

All: We are the people of the major continents of the world. We love life and offer praise to the Lord of our lives.

Leader: Praise be to God, the Lord of all the peoples of earth.

Africa: We are Africa, a continent filled with beauty and promise, pain and poverty. We yearn to be free.

Asia: Burdened with masses of hungry people, we, Asia, cry for the bread of heaven and the bread of earth.

Europe: Once mighty in the eyes of the world, and now the most densely populated of the continents, we, Europe, seek economic stability.

South America: Rapidly growing in people and poverty, we of South America look to our neighbors to the north, east, and west.

North America: We are on top of the world. We in North America possess many things, and yet we are anxious about our dependence upon the exports of the rest of the world to maintain our lifestyle.

All: Praise be to God, the lord of all the peoples of the earth.

Leader: How many of you are there on your continent?

Africa: 17 percent of the people in the world live in Africa.

Asia: Nearly 60 percent of the people in the world live in Asia.

Europe: Almost 10 percent of the people in the world live in Europe.

South America: 6 percent of the people in the world live in South America.

North America: Only 7 percent of the people in the world live in North America.

Leader: Do you people have enough to eat, to eat well?

Africa: 20 percent of people in Africa are hungry.

Asia: 11 percent of Asia's population is undernourished.

South America: 6 percent of people in South America need more to eat.

Australia/Oceania: 6 percent of the population in Australia and Oceania goes without adequate food.

Europe and North America: We, in North America and Europe, have the lowest population count but consume the greatest amount of food; only two percent of our people go hungry.

Leader: This unequal distribution is the cause of the undernourishment and starvation in God's world and it should be the concern of all Christians. What can we do?

All: Perhaps the nations that have more than enough food will share with those who don't have enough. Perhaps businesses can help developing countries solve their own problems by sharing technology and resources. Perhaps churches can give more to help hungry people help themselves. Perhaps we all can make decisions to help our hungry world help itself.

Church World Service Office on Global Education (Tom Hampson, Sandi McFadden, Phyllis Vos Wezeman, and Loretta Whalen). *Make a World of Difference: Creative Activities for Global Learning.* New York, NY: Friendship Press, 1990. Adapted with permission.

I WAS THIRSTY

In the Greek language, the word thirsty is often translated as desperate. Thirst is a strong desire or craving that does not go away until it is satisfied. Physical thirst is usually appeased when a person drinks some type of liquid. Emotional and spiritual thirst must be quenched in other ways.

Ten lessons in this chapter seek to define what it means to be thirsty physically, emotionally, and spiritually. Since Jesus commended the simple act of giving a thirsty person something to drink, Matthew 25:35, experiences in this chapter offer the participants ways to share both their literal and symbolic cups of water with others.

Chart

Lesson	Scripture	Theme	Activity/Method	Page
Overview	▸ Matthew 25:35b, 37b, 42b, 44a	▸ Thirsty		51
Thirsting for God	▸ Psalm 42:1-2 ▸ Jeremiah 17:7-8 ▸ Matthew 5:6	▸ Physical Thirst/ Spiritual Thirst	▸ Art: Sponge Print Card ▸ Culinary: Pretzels/Water ▸ Game: Puddle Hop ▸ Music: "The Tree Song"	54
Appreciating Water	▸ Genesis 1:1-10	▸ Conservation	▸ Art: Chalk Mural ▸ Creative Writing: Five Word Poems	57
Quenching a Thirst	▸ Genesis 24:43-46	▸ Ministering in Jesus' Name	▸ Art: Origami Cup ▸ Clown/Mime: Care & Care-less Skit	60
Discovering Water Facts	▸ Genesis 5:1-9:17 ▸ Exodus 14:1-21 ▸ Isaiah 41:17 ▸ Jonah 1-2 ▸ Matthew 3:17 ▸ John 2:1-11	▸ Experiences and Facts related to water topics	▸ Game: Buckets/Ten Categories	63
Refreshing Water Themes	▸ Psalm 1:3	▸ Physical, Emotional, and Spiritual Refreshment/ Renewal	▸ Game: Bags/Objects ▸ Music: Listen/Play/Write Songs	74
Praising God for Water	▸ Psalm 65:9-10	▸ Appreciation for Water/ Commitment to Conservation	▸ Art: 3-D display on water themes ▸ Creative Writing: A-Z Poems/Prayers	77
Exploring Pollution Problems	▸ Exodus 15:23	▸ Water Pollution Problems/ Solutions	▸ Game: Tray of Objects ▸ Puppetry: Balloon Rod Puppet	80

Living Water	▶ Genesis 1:1-2; 9-10	▶ Jesus is the Living Water	▶ Creative Writing: Picture Booklet	83
	▶ Deuteronomy 8:7-9		▶ Photography: Picture Booklet	
	▶ Psalm 1:1-3			
	▶ Psalm 23:1-2			
	▶ Psalm 41:1-2a			
	▶ Psalm 65:9-10			
	▶ Isaiah 35:5-7			
	▶ Isaiah 41:17-20			
	▶ Isaiah 58:11			
	▶ Matthew 3:11			
	▶ John 4:7-15			
	▶ John 7:37-38			
	▶ John 13:3-5			
	▶ Revelation 7:15-17			
Flowing with Justice	▶ Amos 5:24	▶ Justice and Righteousness	▶ Creative Writing: Litany	86
Filling a Cup in Jesus' Name	▶ Mark 9:41	▶ Serving in Jesus' Name	▶ Art: Clay Cup	89

Thirsting for God

Matthew 5:6

Blessed are those who hunger and thirst for righteousness, for they will be filled.

Learn

Participants will experience physical thirst and explore spiritual thirst as they sample food, listen to music, play a game, and paint cards.

Locate

- Bags or table covering, blue plastic or blue paper
- Basin or sink
- Basket for pretzels
- Bible
- Containers for paint and for water
- Covering for table such as newspaper or recycled plastic dry-cleaning bags
- Cups
- Ice
- Equipment to play recorded music
- Glasses, two
- Markers
- Music for "The Tree Song" by Ken Medema
- Napkins
- Paint, tempera – variety of colors
- Paper, cover stock and plain
- Pens
- Plants, one healthy and one wilted
- Pretzels, salted

- Recordings of joyful music
- Scissors
- Smocks or protective covering for clothing (optional)
- Sponges
- Tape, masking
- Towels, paper or wash cloths
- Water
- Watering can (optional)

Advance Preparation

- Cover two glasses with plain paper. Write the word "God" on one. Fill one or more pitchers with ice water. If a sink is not available, place a basin nearby.

- Obtain the music to "The Tree Song" by Ken Medema. It is available on many internet sites and from: Brier Patch Music 4324 Canal SW, Grandville, MI 49418, (616) 534-6571, www.kenmedema.com.

- Create a game area in a classroom or gathering space. Cut five or six large puddle-shaped pieces of blue "water" from plastic bags, tablecloths, or paper. Use masking tape to affix the shapes to the floor. Set up an area to play joyful songs during the activity.

- Set up a painting area on one or more tables. Cover the table(s) with newspaper or recycled dry cleaning bags. Set out smocks, wet cloths or paper towels, and cover stock paper which has been folded into card shapes. Cut sponges into squares, circles, and other shapes. Pour tempera paint into shallow containers. Make a sample sponge painted card.

Lead

A thirst for God is a very difficult concept for many people, especially children, to understand. And yet, it is as basic and as important a need as the physical necessity for water. In this activity the need for water will be explored in several ways and then linked to the spiritual need for God. A sponge painting activity will result in a card which can be shared with someone who has helped the participants meet a spiritual thirst.

Greet the participants as they arrive, offering them salted pretzels from a basket. Do not give them anything to drink until later in the activity. As they eat, talk about thirst. Ask the group questions like: When have you felt thirsty? What does thirst feel like? Challenge the students to name things that indicate thirst. Ideas might include:

▶ animals – pant;
▶ land – gets dusty, splits;
▶ leather – cracks;
▶ people - ask for a drink, get dry mouth;
▶ plants - wilt;
▶ wood - dries out.

Show the group two plants: one that is healthy and one that is not. Ask the learners to state how the plants are different and to suggest reasons for the differences. Talk about what will happen to the wilting plant if it is not given water. Allow one or more people to help water the plants, especially the dying one. Remark that some plants respond very quickly to water and the wilting one may show a difference by the end of the lesson.

Read Matthew 5:6 and Psalm 42:1-2 to the group. Remark that just as water is necessary for physical life, God is essential for spiritual life. People who are without God are just as thirsty spiritually as people without water are thirsty physically. It is impossible to have spiritual health and a fulfilled life without God. Many people feel a need inside, but they don't know how to quench it. They desperately look for the love, joy, and peace which they need, but they look in all the wrong places to find it.

Show the group a glass which has been covered with plain paper. This glass should be empty, but do not make that obvious to the students. Ask the learners to suggest things people search for to make them feel happy. Write the ideas, such as clothes, money, and the latest thing advertised, on the glass. When the group has run out of ideas ask if the things named quench people's thirst and make them feel satisfied. Turn over the glass and try to pour out its contents. Talk about the fact that it is empty. Discuss that people still feel empty when they look for love, joy, and peace in the wrong places.

Next hold up the glass on which the word "God" is written. This glass should be full of water. Ask the students what people find when they search for God. Record their ideas on the glass. These may include a friend who is always there, a sense of safety, a feeling of joy, or the knowledge that they are loved. Ask the group if people find what they are looking for when they look for God. Pour the contents of the glass into a sink or basin. Emphasize that God is always ready to fill our needs. Produce the pitcher of water and tell the participants that God has plenty of love and joy in reserve and will never run out! Supply additional cups or glasses and offer water to the students. Enjoy how good it tastes.

Ask the students how God always has what we need. Read Jeremiah 17:7-8. A tree that is planted by water will never dry out. People who plant their lives in God, and put their trust in God, will always have the spiritual water which they need. Look at the plants again to see the differences between the two and to see if the water is beginning to help the wilted one.

Play or sing "The Tree Song" by Ken Medema. This song traces the lives of three trees and emphasizes that each remains strong and grows when it is planted in the right place. Assure the participants that God will always be with them. Encourage them to stay close to the source of the water God offers, just like the tree planted by the water.

Play a game to emphasize this truth. Move to the game area where several "puddles" of water are dotted throughout "dry" areas. Instruct the participants to move about the game area while the music is playing. When the music stops, they should move to a blue space as quickly as possible, if they are not already touching one. As the game continues, see if anyone discovers that if they stay on or very near blue places at all times, they will already be there when the music stops. Point out this truth if the students do not discover it first. Do not eliminate participants who are not touching blue. Encourage those who are on a blue puddle to make a space for the others to join them.

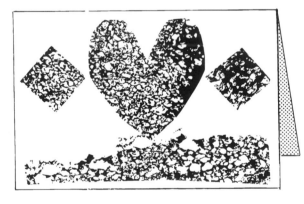

Show the learners a dry sponge. Let them feel how hard and unusable it is. Then dip the sponge into water, remove it, and wring it out slightly. Allow the participants to touch the wet sponge. Remark that when the sponge absorbed the water it became usable again. Make the comparison that if we absorb all that God offers us, we quench our spiritual thirst.

Move to the painting table(s). Demonstrate how to dip a sponge into paint and to blot it on the paper to make a design. Show the cover stock paper that has been folded into card shapes. Instruct the artists to use this process to create designs such as flowers, hearts, trees, or water on the front of a card. Allow each person to make as many cards as time allows. When the cards are completed, set them aside to dry.

Gather the group and ask the participants to name people who have helped them quench their spiritual thirst—or stay close to God. Also ask if there is someone who they would like to help know about God. Encourage the students to send the cards they created, in either of these categories, to these people. Suggest that they write a thank you note to a parent, pastor, or teacher. Note that a loving card written to an uncle or aunt, neighbor or friend, classmate or team player, can help the recipient experience God's love through the sender. If possible, take time to complete this activity during the session.

Once all activities are completed, conclude the lesson by singing or listening to the "The Tree Song" once again.

Appreciating Water

Genesis 1:10a

God called the dry land Earth, and the waters that were gathered together he called Seas.

Learn

Participants will learn to value clean water as they participate in art and creative writing projects that emphasize the theme of conservation.

Locate

- ▶ Basket
- ▶ Bible
- ▶ Chalk, various shades of "water" colors
- ▶ Chalkboard or large sheet of mural paper
- ▶ Markers, dark colors
- ▶ Paper, plain and scrap
- ▶ Pencils
- ▶ Pens
- ▶ Tape, masking

Advance Preparation

- ▶ If mural paper is used, tape it to a wall or place it on a table or on the floor.

Lead

Water is a wonderful and necessary part of God's creation. Unfortunately, it is a gift that can easily be contaminated or wasted. Due to a wide variety of factors, including carelessness and climate, water is not always as available, plentiful, or usable as it should be. In this activity, involving art and creative writing, the participants will talk about ways water is wasted. They will also express an appreciation for water, realizing not everyone has plenty of clean, free-flowing water, and make a commitment to be better stewards of God's precious gift.

Place a basket of chalk near the entrance to the activity space. As the class members arrive, invite them to help create a mural of water on a chalkboard or paper. Make sure everyone has an opportunity to contribute to the joint project. As the students draw, talk about experiences with water like a trip to the beach, share stories about playing at a water park, or discuss favorite attributes of water, such as its refreshing qualities.

When everyone has arrived and the mural is complete, gather the group and read Genesis 1:6-10, the story of Creation. Distribute a piece of white paper to each person. Instruct the students to use chalk to draw their own version of the water which God created. Ask the participants to close their eyes and to think about what that water might have been like. Ask questions such as, What color was it? What did it look like? Was it bubbly, flowing, still, or swirling? How was it different from the water we see today? Tell the group to use their imagination while working with colors and shapes on the page. Instruct them to fill the entire paper with "water." Encourage the artists to experiment with texture, showing them a few examples such as short, dark dashes made with the point of the chalk and wide, flowing strokes done with the side. Provide extra sheets of paper for students who work quickly or who would like to draw more than one picture. Allow time for them to experiment, focusing on what God intended water to be like. When the allotted time is up, set the pictures aside.

Return to the group mural created earlier. Brainstorm all the ways which people waste water. Using a dark color of chalk or marker, write the participants' ideas on top of the drawing, either as a list or scattered in different directions on all parts of the surface. The writing may be done by the leader or students could take turns working as the scribes. This is a good time to emphasize that many people in various parts of the world do not have enough clean water to meet their daily needs.

At the top of the mural, write a caption or statement developed by the group to tie the ideas together. Challenge the students to think of one or two ways they personally waste water and ask them to make a commitment to work at changing their behavior. These ideas could later be written at the top of the individual water drawings.

In the next part of the activity, it is important to guide the participants through the steps without announcing that they will be writing poems. Some people will resist participating and others will freeze, feeling they are not capable of doing a creative writing project. However, following this process, anyone can write a great poem about water in a very simple way. In fact, very young children can compose these poems by telling their water words to someone who writes them down.

Provide scrap paper and pencils for the participants. Ask them to make a list of five words which describe water. After their lists are complete, tell them to write a summary sentence or statement about water at the bottom of the list. For example, the five words and the summary statement might be:

► Bubbling

► Cool

► Flowing

► Refreshing

► Smooth

► Water makes me new again.

Older students can be challenged to add descriptive phrases after each word on their lists. The sample poem could be expanded as follows:

> Bubbling as it runs over me,
> Cool against my hands and face,
> Flowing all around me,
> Refreshing pouring over me,
> Smooth as I run my hands over it,
> Water makes me new again.

Congratulate the writers on their water poems. Distribute the individual chalk drawings of water to each artist. Provide pens or markers and direct them to write their poems on top of their drawings. When complete, sit in a circle on the floor, with each person holding his or her own poem and drawing. Share the pages in one of several ways. Hold them up, showing them to the other group members. Place them on a bulletin board or display, where they can be viewed by everyone. Take turns reading the poems or having them read by a leader. Older students can pass the poems from person to person, allowing a designated amount of time for the students to read a poem silently and then passing it to the next person when the signal is given. This is a very non-threatening way of sharing the writing, since it is nearly impossible to keep track of whose poem is being read. It will also help the learners to experience a wide variety of ways of picturing and describing God's wonderful gift of water.

Complete the activity by spending a few moments in quietness. Ask the participants to return to their imaginings of what God created water to be like. Then ask them to remember their own way(s) of wasting water. Tell the learners to ask God to help them follow through with a commitment to change one or more wasteful habit. End with the participants silently reviewing their own poems, using them as a prayer of thanksgiving to God for water.

Quenching a Thirst

Genesis 24:43

I am standing here by the spring of water; ...I shall say, 'Please give me a little water from your jar to drink'...

Learn

Participants will discover ways to minister in Jesus' name as they create an origami cup and use it in a clown skit.

Locate

- ► Bible
- ► Containers for water, two
- ► Hats, various styles
- ► Paint, water color – various colors
- ► Paint brushes
- ► Paper, freezer wrap type cut into eight-inch squares
- ► Pencils or pens
- ► Pitcher
- ► Scissors
- ► Stickers, red
- ► Water

Advance Preparation

- ► Cut freezer wrap paper into eight-inch squares, one per person.

Lead

In the Bible, offering a cup of cold water to a thirsty person is likened unto ministering to Jesus himself. Every day, week, month, and year there are countless opportunities—literally and symbolically - to share this life sustaining substance with others. In this activity, participants will create an origami drinking cup and use it as a prop in a clown skit. The skit is based on the New Testament theme of servanthood, the underlying philosophy of the biblical directive to share a cup of cold water and to minister to others in Jesus' name.

Introduce the activity by helping each learner make an origami drinking cup. Origami is the Japanese art of paper folding. Distribute eight-inch squares of sturdy freezer wrap paper, making sure the waxed surface is facing up. Guide the group in the following steps:

- ► fold the paper in half diagonally to form a triangle.
- ► fold the left-hand corner to the middle of the opposite edge.
- ► fold the right-hand corner to the middle of the opposite edge.

Note that there are two layers of paper that form the triangle at the top of the cup. Fold the top layer forward and the other layer back. The cup is complete and ready to use as a drinking glass.

When the projects are completed, invite the group to take their cups and to gather in a circle on chairs or on the floor. Read Genesis

24:43-46 about Abraham's servant's need for a drink of water. Tell the group that they will be preparing and presenting a clown skit in which they will play the parts of thirsty people. Note that they will be writing two words on their cups - one will be a type of person who might be thirsty such as child, older woman, or teenager. The other word will be a place where a person in need of water could be found such as hospital, war-torn country, or sports field. Brainstorm a list of people and places. Distribute pens or pencils and direct each student to write a different type of person on one side of the cup and a specific place on the other side. Help each pupil match the two themes, such as older person in a nursing home or teenager on an athletic field and write the words on the cup. Strive for as much variety, and reality, as possible. Remind the participants that the words written on their cups tell them the characters they will portray in the clown skit.

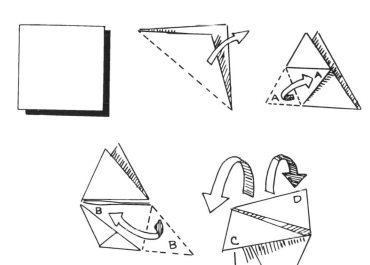

Create "Quick Clowns" by asking the learners to change three things about their clothing. Suggest ideas like rolling up one pant leg, putting a shirt on backwards, and wearing shoes on the wrong feet. If hats are available, let each person choose one to wear. Place a red circle sticker on everyone's nose to signify the mark of the clown. If time allows, provide water color paints, water, and brushes, and have each person think of a simple design to

paint on his or her cheek to symbolize the character or the concept they wish to convey during the skit.

Set the scene by explaining the basic premise of the story. Two clowns, "Care" and "Care-less," set off on a journey. Each clown carries a container of water which holds just enough of this necessity to last throughout the trip. Along the way Care and Care-less meet various people who are thirsty and in need of a drink of water. Care always shares from the limited supply and the water never runs out. Care-less does not share. Care-less not only drinks the water but also wastes it by spilling it while stumbling over obstacles in the road. As the two clowns meet people along the path, the thirsty ones must communicate, verbally or non-verbally, to describe the character they represent and their need for a drink. Care responds by sharing water while Care-less reacts in ways that waste or consume the water. When everyone understands the instructions, remind the players that they are to spontaneously act out their parts and possible responses during the skit.

Position the thirsty people throughout a path in the room. Proceed with the clown skit. Near the end of the path, or activity, Care-less should be completely out of water and act thirsty and Care, together with the other clowns, must decide what to do about it.

At the end of the activity, discuss the attitudes and actions expressed during the exercise considering the scriptural principles previously explored. Remind the students that they are called to be servants, caretakers, and stewards of the many gifts God has given to them - including water. Re-gather the group in a circle and ask each person to hold up the cup. Surprise the actors by producing a pitcher of water and pouring a small amount of it into each cup. Celebrate and drink the water together. Distribute another square of paper to each person. Challenge the group to take the paper home and to use it to make a cup to give to someone else. Both cups can serve as reminders to minister to others in Jesus' name, even with something as common as water.

Discovering Water Facts

Isaiah 41:17
When the poor and needy seek water, and there is none, and their tongue is parched with thirst, I the Lord will answer them, I the God of Israel will not forsake them.

Learn

Participants will play a bucket game to explore ten topics related to water themes.

Locate

- Bibles
- Buckets, ten
- Chalk, sidewalk type (optional)
- Copy machine or printer
- Dice, spinner, or numbered slips of paper
- Game marker pieces such as buttons or drop-shaped paper
- Glasses
- Items for Water Conservation bucket: hand broom, laundry detergent bottle, rubber washer, seed packet, and shower nozzle
- Markers, permanent
- Markers, washable
- Newsprint, poster board, or recycled white bed sheet
- Paper for copy machine or printer
- Paper cutter or scissors
- Pitcher
- Resource sheet: "Discovering Water Facts Game Board"
- Resource sheet: "Discovering Water Facts Game Cards"
- Water

Advance Preparation

- Prepare ten buckets for the game. Label each bucket with one of the following categories:
  - Water Concerns
  - Water Conservation
  - Water Cycle
  - Water Facts
  - Water Memories
  - Water Pollution
  - Water Projects
  - Water Scripture Stories/Verses
  - Water Songs
  - Water Uses
- Prepare one large Discovering Water Facts game board for the entire group to use. Using the outline on the resource sheet as a guide, reproduce it on large pieces of paper or on a recycled white bed sheet. To play the game outside, use chalk to draw the game board on a sidewalk or on the pavement of a parking lot.

► Copy the Discovering Water Facts game cards, cut them apart, and place them in the appropriate buckets.

► For the Water Conversation bucket, place the following items in it: hand broom, laundry detergent bottle, rubber washer, seed packet, and shower nozzle.

► For the Water Scripture Stories/Verses bucket, place a Bible in the container in addition to the game cards.

► Duplicate copies of the Discovering Water Facts Game Board resource sheet for the participants to take home.

► Obtain information from organizations about world-wide water projects. Contact places such as:

Catholic Relief Services
228 W. Lexington Street
Baltimore, MD 21201-3443
877-435-7211
www.crs.org

Church World Service
28606 Phillips Street
Elkhart, IN 46514
800-297-1516
www.cwsglobal.org

Lead

Water is a worldwide need and a worldwide concern. In the United States, most people turn on a faucet and treated, drinkable water flows out of it. In many parts of the world, water—often unclean—must be drawn and carried from a stream, well, or spring. In many countries women do most of the water bearing, sometimes spending several hours each day obtaining this resource for their families. Learning about water issues around the world is a serious matter but the method used to discover facts and figures can be done in a fun way. Play a game to help the participants explore several themes related to water. Some of the categories are based on facts and some relate to personal opinions and experiences. The directions provided suggest playing the game cooperatively using one large game board. Participants are also offered the opportunity to take individual game sheets home to repeat the activity with family and friends.

Begin by telling the group that they will be playing a game related to water. Explain that ten categories will be used, and players will have the opportunity to read a fact, answer a

question, offer a response, or share an experience for each of them. Refer to the ten labeled buckets. Ask the group to guess why buckets are used in this game. Of course, buckets are one method of carrying water. Provide information on ways some people in the world obtain their water by walking great distances and carrying small amounts of the precious resource back to their homes in bucket-like containers. Read the words on each bucket and explain the ten themes that will be used in this activity.

- **Water Concerns**: Pupils will answer yes or no to a water concern question.

- **Water Conservation**: Participants will name one method of conserving water.

- **Water Cycle**: Players will answer true or false to statements about the water cycle.

- **Water Facts**: Learners will read a fact about water.

- **Water Memories**: Students will share a memory of a water experience.

- **Water Pollution**: Pupils will select a correct answer from a multiple-choice question related to pollution.

- **Water Projects**: Students will read information about a water related project taking place in the world.

- **Water Scripture Stories/Verses**: Participants will name or recite a scripture verse or story related to water.

- **Water Songs**: Players will tell the name of a song related to water.

- **Water Uses**: Learners will suggest uses of water.

Get ready to play the game! Try it in a cooperative format by using one large game board on the floor or wall inside or on a sidewalk or parking lot outside and having all students participate. Explain that each person, in turn, will throw one die, use a spinner, or pick a slip of paper containing a number from one to six. The numeral indicates the number of spaces the player moves on that turn. When the player physically walks to the space, or marks it with an object, he or she calls out the category. The player may choose one card, or item, from that bucket and share the information on it with the group. If an answer is required the player may supply it, however help from the rest of the group is expected and encouraged.

Before beginning the game, review the activities and the directions for each bucket.

Water Concerns

Players will answer a yes or no question on an important concern or issue involving water. The player who lands on this space selects one card from the bucket, reads the question to the group, gives a yes or no answer, or asks for help from the group to make the response.

Answers:

1. No
2. Yes
3. Yes
4. Yes
5. Yes

Water Conservation

Participants name one method of conserving water. The player who lands on this space picks one item from the bucket and names a method of conserving water related to it.

For example:

▶ hand broom – sweep sidewalks instead of hosing them;

▶ laundry detergent bottle – run full rather than partial loads of clothes;

▶ rubber washer – repair leaky faucets;

▶ seed packet – collect rain water to nourish plants;

▶ shower nozzle – take shorter showers.

Water Cycle

Students answer true or false statements about the water cycle. The player who lands on this space draws one card, reads it aloud, answers the question, or asks for help from the other participants to make a response.

Answers:

1. True
2. False
3. True
4. True
5. False

Water Facts

Pupils read a fact about water. The player who lands on this space draws one card and reads the statement to the group.

Water Memories

Contestants share a memory of an experience related to water. The player who lands on this place draws one card, reads the statement to the group, and relates a personal experience based on the suggestion.

Water Pollution

Learners select a correct answer to a multiple-choice question about water pollution. The player who lands on this space draws one card, reads the question to the group, selects an answer, or asks for help from the other participants to make a response.

Answers:

1. b
2. c
3. c
4. a
5. c

Water Projects

Students read information about a current water-related project or organization that is active in the world. The player who lands on this space draws one card from the bucket and reads the statement to the group.

Water Scripture Stories/Verses

Players recite a Bible verse or share a Scripture story related to water. A player who lands on this place draws one card, reads the Scripture reference written on it, looks up the passage in a Bible, and reads the verse or paraphrases the story for the group.

Water Songs

Students sing songs with water-themed lyrics and titles. The player who lands on this space picks one card from the bucket, sings the song, and challenges the group to name the title. The player may ask for an adult leader or another student or two to help sing the song.

As an alternative to singing the songs, the player may try to elicit the title from the other participants. This could be done through pantomime or by drawing a space for each letter and playing a game of Hangman.

Water Uses

Players suggest a general or a specific use for water. The player who lands on this space draws one card, reads the category, and gives a general use for water related to the topic. For example, a water use for farming could be irrigation or a water use for recreation might be surfing.

~

Continue the game until each person has had at least one turn. When the activity is concluded, reward the group for their efforts by offering them cool, refreshing glasses of water.

In conclusion, distribute copies of the game to take home. Suggest that the students share the activity with family and friends using questions and statements they research and develop on their own.

Discovering Water Facts Game Board

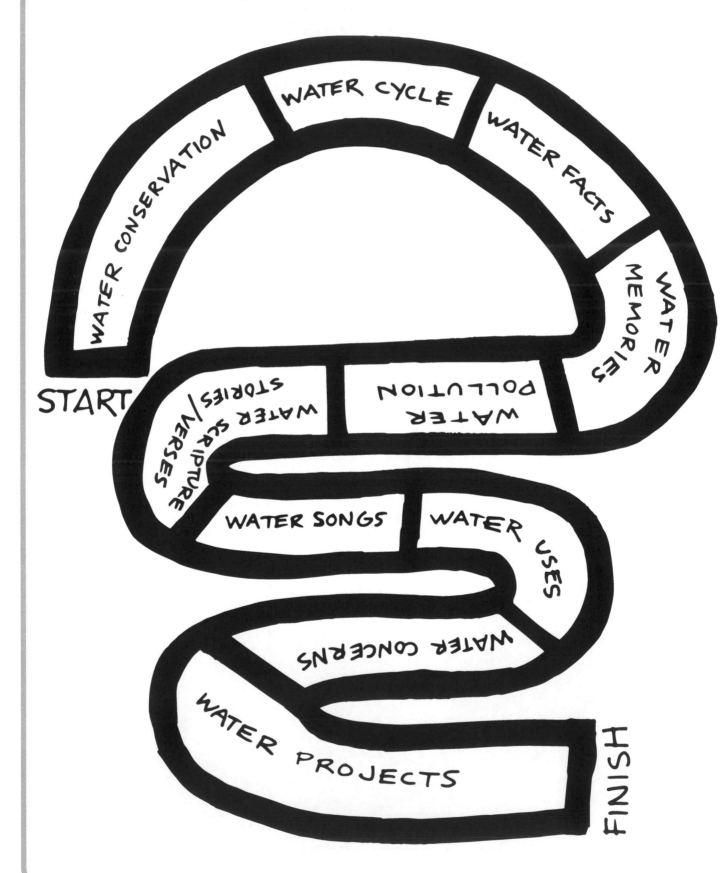

START

WATER CONSERVATION

WATER CYCLE

WATER FACTS

WATER MEMORIES

WATER POLLUTION

WATER SCRIPTURE STORIES/VERSES

WATER SONGS

WATER USES

WATER CONCERNS

WATER PROJECTS

FINISH

Seeing Jesus

Discovering Water Facts Game Cards

Water Concerns #1	Water Cycle #1
Do all people in the world have access to clean water?	True or False? Hydro is a Greek word that means water.
Water Concerns #2	**Water Cycle #2**
Do children become sick because they do not have water to drink?	True or False? Water is recycled once a week.
Water Concerns #3	**Water Cycle #3**
Is diarrhea a water related illness in some countries?	True or False? Water appears in three states: liquid, solid, and gas.
Water Concerns #4	**Water Cycle #4**
If people do not have water to wash themselves can they become sick?	True or False? Transpiration is the process by which plants and animals give off water vapor.
Water Concerns #5	**Water Cycle #5**
Is infant death related to unhealthy water standards in some countries?	True or False? All water goes through the water cycle at the same time and rate.

Discovering Water Facts Game Cards

Water Fact #1 More than 1,000,000 gallons of water are needed to make an automobile.	**Water Memory #1** Tell about one time you had fun in water.
Water Fact #2 A cow needs three gallons of water to produce a gallon of milk.	**Water Memory #2** Share one experience of thirst.
Water Fact #3 It takes 1,400 gallons of water to grow and process the ingredients for a hamburger, fries, and soft drink.	**Water Memory #3** Talk about a time water helped transport you from one place to another.
Water Fact #4 It is estimated that 25,000 people die each day at least due in part to the lack of clean drinking water.	**Water Memory #4** Tell about one time you needed water and didn't have any.
Water Fact #5 Eighty percent of all sickness and disease in the world can be attributed to inadequate water and sanitation.	**Water Memory #5** Describe one way you've used water for health-related purposes.

Discovering Water Facts Game Cards

## Water Pollution #1	## Water Projects #1

Balloons cause danger to marine animals because the animals think the balloons are:
    a. toys
    b. food
    c. shelter
	World relief organizations provide tools and construction materials to dig wells in underdeveloped countries.

## Water Pollution #2	## Water Projects #2

Plastic rings that hold six packs of cans together should be:
    a. left on the beach
    b. thrown in the garbage
    c. snipped before being thrown away
	Systems of pumping water to storage tanks are being developed in many countries of the world.

## Water Pollution #3	## Water Projects #3

Chemical spills in oceans affect:
    a. people
    b. marine life
    c. both
	New irrigation techniques result in increased food crops in many areas.

## Water Pollution #4	## Water Projects #4

Fertilizers are most dangerous when they contaminate:
    a. ground water
    b. hands
    c. bushes
	Percolation (draining or oozing) dams filter the water into the soil below, helping to raise the water table.

## Water Pollution #5	## Water Projects #5

Major pollutants in oceans include:
    a. oil
    b. untreated sewage
    c. both
	Fish farms are being developed to supplement the diets of many people.

Discovering Water Facts Game Cards

Water Scripture Stories/Verses #1	Water Songs #1
Exodus 14:1-21 - Moses and the parting of the Red Sea	"Raindrops Keep Falling on My Head"

Water Scripture Stories/Verses #2	Water Songs #2
Genesis 5:1-9:17 - Noah and the ark	"Rain, Rain, Go Away"

Water Scripture Stories/Verses #3	Water Songs #3
Jonah 1-2 - Jonah and the whale	"I've Got Peace Like a River"

Water Scripture Stories/Verses #4	Water Songs #4
John 2:1-11 - Jesus' first miracle - changing water into wine	"Peace Is Flowing Like a River"

Water Scripture Stories/Verses #5	Water Songs #5
Matthew 3:17 - Jesus' baptism in the Jordan River	"Wide, Wide as the Ocean"

Discovering Water Facts Game Cards

Water Use #1 Cleaning
Water Use #2 Drinking
Water Use #3 Farming
Water Use #4 Medicinal
Water Use #5 Recreation

Refreshing Water Themes

Psalm 1:3

They are like trees planted by streams of water, which yield their fruit in its season, and their leaves do not wither. In all that they do, they prosper.

Learn

Participants will play a game involving objects and use music to explore ways water refreshes people physically, emotionally, and spiritually.

Locate

- ▶ Bags or boxes, one for each object
- ▶ Bible
- ▶ Equipment to play music
- ▶ Markers, pencils, or pens
- ▶ Objects associated with water's renewing qualities, such as:
  - ▶ Bathing suit or swimming trunks
  - ▶ Boat toy
  - ▶ Glass or pitcher
  - ▶ Hose or nozzle
  - ▶ Pet dish
  - ▶ Sprinkling can
  - ▶ Squirt gun
  - ▶ Vase
  - ▶ Wash cloth
- ▶ Paper
- ▶ Recording of music with water themed lyrics and titles

Advance Preparation

- ▶ Place one object related to water's refreshing qualities in each bag or box.

Lead

One of water's greatest qualities is the way that it refreshes. A glass of ice water on a hot day quenches thirst; a gentle rainfall revives wilting plants; a thorough scrubbing revitalizes well-worn buildings. Because of this unique quality of renewal, water is often used as a symbol of spiritual refreshment. Psalm 1:3 states that people who trust in God, just like trees planted by streams, are revitalized. This activity emphasizes the need for physical, emotional, and spiritual refreshment and highlights music with a water theme as one method of attaining this renewal.

There are many objects that can relate to water's important quality of renewal. Help the participants explore this concept by using a game involving bags or boxes which contain actual items related to this theme.

Distribute the bags, which were prepared in advance, except for the one containing the water-related music. One bag may be given to each participant or small group or they may be issued randomly to individuals in the class. Ask each person, one at a time, to remove the object in the bag and to name it. Once all of the items have been displayed, challenge the students to state what they have in common. Naturally, they will say that they are all connected with water. Ask them to be more exact and to identify one specific quality of water associated with the items. The idea is that the objects all have something to do with water's quality of renewal and refreshment. Take turns looking at each object and stating how it can be used to renew or refresh someone or something.

For example:

- **Bathing suit or swimming trunks**: Swim on a hot day
- **Boat**: Take a relaxing ride
- **Glass or pitcher**: Give a drink of water
- **Nozzle or hose**: Water garden or lawn
- **Pet dish**: Revive an animal
- **Sprinkling can**: Water plants
- **Squirt gun**: Play a fun game
- **Vase**: Keep flowers alive
- **Wash cloth**: Clean a dirty face

Produce the last bag and remove the recording of water-themed music. Ask the group to suggest what music has to do with water's important quality of refreshment. Discuss the fact that all people have physical, emotional, and spiritual thirsts. Everyone needs to be renewed in body, mind, and spirit. Music is one method many people use to revive and revitalize themselves.

Invite the participants to listen to different kinds of music with water-related themes. Play recordings which range from calypso to classical, rag to rock, and pop to polka. Suggestions include, but are not limited to:

Choruses

- "The Joy of the Lord Is My Strength"
- "Wide, Wide as the Ocean"

Classical

- "The Moldau" (Smetena)
- "Water Music" (Handel)

Folk

- "A Hard Rain's 'Gonna Fall" (Bob Dylan)
- "Big River" (Grateful Dead)

Guided Meditation

- "Like a River" (LuraMedia)

Hymns

- "Ho, Everyone That Thirsteth"
- "Peace Is Flowing Like a River"

Musicals

- "Big River"
- "Down by the Creekbank"

Pop

- "Raindrops Keep Falling on My Head"
- "Somewhere Over the Rainbow"

Religious Recordings

- "As Water to the Thirsty" (David Haas)
- "Come to the Water" (Marty Haugen)

Sound Tapes

- Mountain Streams
- Thunderstorm

Soundtrack

- "Water Gift of Life" (The Nature Company)

After playing a variety of music explore with the students how the music makes them feel. Does fast, peppy music help them feel happy? Does slow, solemn music make them sad? What type makes them feel calm and peaceful? Encourage the participants to share their feelings with the group. Assure them that it is alright for everyone to have different responses and reactions.

In addition to listening to music, involve the group in a variety of other music-related activities. Try making music by filling jars or glasses with different levels of water and creating sounds by taping the containers. Write new words to a familiar tune such as "Jesus Loves Me." For example:

Verse

> Water helps me feel cool
> after I've played at home or school.
> Thank You God for this great gift
> that always gives me such a lift!

Chorus

> Thanks, God, for water.
> Thanks, God, for water.
> Thanks, God, for water -
> the gift of life to me.

Conclude the activity by singing or listening to a song thanking God for the ways in which the gift of water refreshes people physically, emotionally, and spiritually.

Praising God for Water

Psalm 65:9

You visit the earth and water it,
you greatly enrich it;
the river of God is full of water;
you provide the people with grain,
for so you have prepared it.

Learn

Participants will express appreciation for God's gift of water as they create an A-Z poem/prayer, make a commitment to conserve this resource, and design a three-dimensional display to focus on these themes.

Locate

- ► Bible
- ► Hole punch
- ► Markers
- ► Material for "clouds" such as fabric, felt, paper tablecloth, pillow cases, plastic bags
- ► Paper, construction or poster board
- ► Paper, newsprint
- ► Pens
- ► Ribbon, string, or yarn
- ► Scissors
- ► Stencil patterns for letters of the alphabet or purchased sets of A to Z letters
- ► Tacks
- ► Tape, duct

Advance Preparation

Cut the letters of the alphabet from construction paper or poster board. As an alternative, purchase sets of A-Z letters.

Prepare three large pieces of newsprint for the introductory activity. Write one of these words in the center of each sheet: Morning, Afternoon, Evening. Hang the posters in the room where everyone can see them.

Lead

Water is the most essential of all life-sustaining elements. The adult human body is composed of approximately sixty percent water. People have been known to live for up to 80 days without food but only a few days without water. To survive a person needs to consume about two quarts of water a day and an individual could drink as much as 15,000 gallons of water in a lifetime. Although water is the most basic resource required, it is, unfortunately, often the one most taken for granted. Through involvement in this prayer activity, participants will thank God for the uses of water in their lives and discover ways to appreciate and conserve this important gift.

As the participants arrive, direct their attention to the three posters containing the words Morning, Afternoon, and Evening. Supply markers and instruct the group to write words or phrases, or to draw pictures, of ways in which they use water at these times during the day. Responses might include: morning—taking a shower, afternoon—cooking macaroni, and evening—brushing teeth. When everyone has gathered, and when many answers have been generated, allow time for the students to share and explain what they wrote.

Hand each person one or more letters of the alphabet. Instruct the group to form a circle, with A at the beginning of the line and Z at the end. Invite the participants to hold the letter they received in front of them. Tell the learners that they will be creating a unique prayer, thanking God for every use of water in their lives. Challenge the group to think of a use for water for every letter of the alphabet. Beginning with the person holding the A, direct each pupil, in turn, to name a use of water that starts with the letter they are holding. Encourage the group to help each other come up with ideas. When everyone understands the procedure, start the prayer with words such as God, we thank you for every use of water. Continue around the circle until everyone has contributed an idea. Suggested words include:

► A - Appliances
► B - Bath
► C - Cooking
► D - Drink
► E - Electricity
► F - Fishing
► G - Gardening
► H - Hospitals
► I - Ice
► J - Juice
► K - Kids
► L - Laundry
► M - Manufacturing
► N - Nuclear Power
► O - Orchards

► P - Plants
► Q - Quarts
► R - Recreation
► S - Swimming
► T - Transportation
► U - Utilities
► V - Vase
► W - Wash
► X - X-ray film developing
► Y - Yards
► Z - Zoos

See how many times the group can go through the alphabet without missing a letter. Conclude the prayer with a group "Amen."

Remind the participants that although water is one of the most essential resources, unfortunately it is also one of the most taken for granted ones. Hold up a globe or a map. Ask the students to guess the percentage of water that covers the earth. The answer is seventy percent. Now ask them to state the percentage of the earth's water that is actually available for use. Ninety-seven percent of the earth's water is saltwater found in the world's seas and oceans. Two percent is trapped in glaciers and ice caps. That leaves only one percent usable water found in lakes, rivers, and underground wells. Although ocean water is desalinated in some places, there is not as much usable drinking water in the world as one might imagine. Also, great amounts of water are wasted. Therefore, it is important to conserve water so there will be enough for everyone in the world. Invite the group to use their letters to think of ways in which water can be conserved. If players trade letters, re-form the circle with the person holding A at the beginning and the individual with Z at the end. Repeat the process of going around the circle, taking turns naming conservation related words beginning with the letters the students are holding. Before using the words in a prayer, explain or expand information about some of the themes and topics that may be new to the participants.

Conservation words for every letter of the alphabet include:

- ► A - Aerators
- ► B - Broom (Sweep instead of hosing off sidewalks)
- ► C - Compost (Rather than use a garbage disposal)
- ► D - Displacement devices
- ► E - Energy
- ► F - Full loads in machines
- ► G - Grass (Cut less often)
- ► H - Hose
- ► I - Instruct
- ► J - Justice issues
- ► K - Knowledge
- ► L - Leaks (Repair)
- ► M - Mulch
- ► N - Nozzles
- ► O - Organizations (Get involved)
- ► P - Pre-soak
- ► Q - Question
- ► R - Repair
- ► S - Short Shower (Rather than bath)
- ► T - Trees (Plant them)
- ► U - Used water (For plants)
- ► V - Views (Share them)
- ► W - Water saving model appliances
- ► X - X-tra
- ► Y - Yards
- ► Z - Zoning

After the group has explored conservation options, lead them in a prayer asking God to help each person do his or her part to conserve water.

Instruct the participants to sit down. Distribute pens or markers and tell the group to write on their letter of the alphabet the words they shared during the two prayer activities. Invite the group to combine their letters and words into a three-dimensional bulletin board or wall hanging. Provide construction paper, scissors, and glue. Direct the students to cut or tear large water drops from the paper and to glue their letter to the center of the shape. Punch a hole in the top of each paper, then thread and tie a length of ribbon, string, or yarn through the hole to form a hanger for the drop.

Challenge the students to cooperate to construct clouds from which to hang the drops. Several methods could be used for forming the clouds, especially creating them from recycled materials. Try tearing white paper tablecloth or newsprint or cutting large sheets of construction paper or poster board into cloud shapes. Fabric that has been sewn together, pillowcases, or plastic bags may be stuffed with newspaper and shaped to form clouds. Materials such as felt or Fiberfill®, if available, also make great clouds. Secure the cloud shapes to a bulletin board, wall, or ceiling with heavy tape or tacks. Allow the participants to attach the top of their strings to the clouds. Admire the cloud creations and read Psalm 65:9-10 to the group. Conclude by inviting the participants to say together, "Thank God for every use of water in my life!"

Exploring Pollution Problems

Exodus 15:23

When they came to Marah, they could not drink the water of Marah because it was bitter.

Learn

Participants will play a memory game to learn about water pollution problems and construct balloon rod puppets to suggest possible solutions.

Locate

- Balloons, large round
- Bible
- Bowl or bucket
- Cardboard strips
- Dowel rods
- Egg cartons
- Fabric
- Glue
- Items for memory game
  - Fishing line
  - Hypodermic needle case
  - Insecticide
  - Lawn Fertilizer
  - Motor oil
  - Oven cleaner
  - Paint can
  - Picture of underground storage tanks
  - Trash
  - Newspaper

- Paint
- Paint brushes
- Paper
- Pencils or pens
- Scissors
- Spoon or stir stick
- Tray
- Wallpaper paste
- Yarn and materials for puppet hair

Advance Preparation

Prepare a tray containing examples or pictures of items related to water pollution:

- P - Paint
- O - Oil (Motor)
- L - Lawn fertilizer
- L - Line (Fishing)
- U - Underground storage tanks
- T - Trash
- I - Insectide
- O - Oven cleaner
- N - Needle

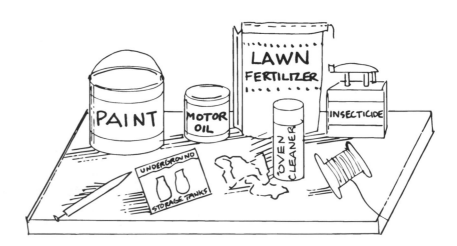

Lead

Clean water is one of the world's most precious resources. Clean water is also something that is often taken for granted. It is estimated that during the twenty-first century as much as one-fourth of the world's reliable water supply could be considered unsafe for use because of pollution. In this activity, participants will play a memory game to consider pollution problems and construct balloon rod puppets to suggest solutions.

As class begins, offer a brief overview of the current problem of water pollution. Pollution is a serious threat to the world's supply of available water. Most water comes from one of two sources: surface water such as lakes and rivers or deep underground aquifers or wells. Both sources are being threatened by the pollution that has become part of everyday life. For example, almost everything that is put on the ground ends up in the water. This includes things like the salts used to de-ice highways, motor oil, and hazardous chemicals stored in municipal landfills. When rain or irrigation water washes across the surface of the land, the toxic substances run into rivers and streams and contaminate them. Pollution causes many problems to humans and marine life including disease, defects, and death.

Read Exodus 15:23 to the group. Without further comment on the scripture passage, pass out a piece of paper and a pencil to each person. Tell the class that they will be shown a tray containing nine examples of objects related to the theme of this Bible verse. Some of the examples will be actual objects while others will be pictures. They will have one minute to study the tray and to memorize the items it contains. After sixty seconds, the tray will be removed, and the participants will have one more minute to write on their papers as many of the items as they can remember. Clarify the procedure and begin the activity. Display the tray of objects for one minute. Remove the tray and time the group as they record their answers for sixty seconds. If additional time is required, provide another minute for each segment of the activity. Review the answers together.

Next, tell the group that the first letters of each of the words can be combined to form another word. Individually, or in small groups, allow time for the participants to come up with the answer: POLLUTION. Explain that pollution is a serious threat to the world's supply of safe water. Show the tray of objects again and note that all of the items on it are things that can pollute water. Take time for discussion about the items and their risks. Ask the students to name additional sources of water pollution. Suggestions include thousands of different types of chemicals, gasoline and other petroleum products; animal wastes from agriculture, pets, and stray animals; construction debris; salts that de-ice highways; industrial pollutants; sediment; and plastics of all sorts. Concentrate on the issue of plastics and the danger this substance poses to the water supply. Plastic has improved people's lives in many ways, but the qualities that have made it so successful - lightweight, durable, and strong - also make plastic debris a persistent threat in oceans and waterways. Marine animals sometimes confuse plastic items for real food. Plastic bags look like jellyfish to sea turtles and plastic six-pack holders are virtually invisible underwater to marine animals. Birds, fish, seals, and other animals get tangled in these and either die of starvation or strangulation. Another plastic pollution problem is balloons. Use a puppetry activity to help the participants learn more about the dangers balloons cause to marine life.

Ask if anyone has participated in a balloon launch. Remark that it's fun to release helium balloons and watch them float out to space. But, outer space isn't really where they go. When the helium is gone the balloons fall back to earth. Most of them end up in the ocean where the saltwater washes off their color and makes them look like jellyfish. Many animals, like sea lions and whales, swallow balloons. Pieces of rubber often get caught in their throats and the animals starve to death. Remind the group that before releasing a balloon people should consider the risks. Invite the group to turn a balloon into a puppet instead of releasing it into the atmosphere and use it to teach others about pollution problems.

Demonstrate the procedure for making a puppet from a balloon. Begin with a balloon, add paper mache, and produce a character. Blow up a large, round balloon, and tie off the end. Tear the newspaper into strips. Mix one cup of paste into ten cups of warm water. Stir until it is well blended. Dip the newspaper pieces into the paste and cover the balloon with two single layers. Make eyes, nose, mouth, ears, wrinkles, and other facial features by gluing cardboard strips, pieces of egg cartons, or other materials to the face. Cover the head with two more layers of the paste covered paper. While the head is drying, carefully insert a dowel rod into the center of the bottom of the puppet. This will be the handle by which it is operated. After the puppet head is dry, paint the head with tempera paint to create the face. Make hair from yarn, cotton, fake fur, feathers, paper curls, garland, or another material. Add a simple costume by sliding a piece of fabric up the rod and taping it into place.

Tell the participants to decide on the character they will construct. It can be a person or an animal. Distribute the supplies and guide the puppet making process. Use this time to talk with individuals about water pollution problems and solutions. Once the puppets are completed, organize the puppet-makers into pairs and challenge them to come up with short skits illustrating pollution themes. For example, one puppet could play the part of a child who wants his or her class to do a balloon release and the other puppet could portray the role of a young person or an adult who explains the problems balloons cause. Have the two people seek a satisfactory solution. If possible, help each group come up with a different topic. Invite the teams to take turns presenting their puppet skits for each other. Challenge the participants to be more aware of pollution problems and solutions.

Living Water

John 4:14
The water that I will give will become in them a spring of water gushing up to eternal life.

Learn

Participants will use scripture selections to explore the theme of Jesus as the Living Water and create a picture booklet to express their understanding of this truth.

Locate

- Bibles
- Binding material such as brads, ribbon, rings, or string
- Calendars, magazines, and travel brochures with pictures of water
- Copy machine or printer
- Equipment to play music
- Hole punch
- Markers
- Music for "Spring Up, O Well" by Phil Wickham
- Paper, construction
- Paper for copy machine or printer
- Pens
- Resource sheet: "Living Water Scripture Verses"
- Scissors

Advance Preparation

Make copies of the Living Water Scripture Verses resource sheet.

Lead

Just as physical water quenches the physical thirst that everyone experiences, spiritual water is necessary to quell the spiritual thirst that people encounter as well. In a conversation with a Samaritan woman, Jesus offered her the gift of spiritual water—water which would be readily available and which would never run out. In John 4:14 Jesus said, "Those who drink of the water that I will give them will never be thirsty. The water that I will give will become in them a spring of water gushing up to eternal life." Spiritual water is the water of life, the water that appeases earthly anxieties and worries. In this activity, the participants will make

a class booklet to help them use words and pictures to express the reality of this life-giving truth.

When the group has gathered, begin the activity by singing the song, "Spring Up, O Well" by Phil Wickham. Emphasize that this spring of Living Water is available to everyone. The lyrics are:

> I've got a river of life flowin' out of me.
> Makes the lame to walk and the blind to see.
> Opens prison doors, sets the captives free.
> I've got a river of life flowin' out of me.
> Spring up Oh Well within my soul.
> Spring up Oh Well and make me whole
> Spring up Oh Well and give to me
> that life abundantly.

Read John 4:13-15 to the group. Discuss the description of Jesus as Living Water. Ask the group questions like: How is Jesus like water? How is Jesus like Living Water? Why is Jesus necessary for life? What difference does Jesus make in your life? Make sure the students understand that just as their bodies cannot live without physical water, their spirits cannot truly live without Jesus and the Living Water which Jesus provides.

To help the students comprehend the abstract concept of Living Water invite them to work together to develop a class picture booklet that illustrates this theme. The first step of the project is to research and read scripture verses that convey the meaning of Living Water. Organize the participants into seven groups. Provide a Bible and a resource sheet, Living Water Scripture Verses, for each team. Assign two passages to each group. Tell the students to look up and read the two verses they were given and to select the one they find most helpful in understanding the concept of Living Water.

Next, assign the participants to choose or create pictures which illustrate their scripture statements. Supply a selection of calendars, magazines, and travel brochures as a source of water pictures. Make sheets of construction paper, glue sticks, markers, pens, and scissors available to share. Tell the learners to cut out their selected images and to use a glue stick to mount them to a piece of colored construction paper. When the illustrations are completed, tell each team to write its Bible verse or phrase on their page.

Invite the group to choose a title for the book and have a few students create a title page. Punch three uniform holes on the left side of the pages of the book. Bind the sheets together using brads, ribbon, rings, or yarn.

Gather the group in a circle on chairs or on the floor, displaying the book so that everyone can see it. Explore the book together, taking turns reading each page. Through sight and sound, allow the pictures and the words to communicate to the participants Jesus' claim to be Living Water. Encourage everyone to hear and to accept Jesus' gift to him or her.

If possible, arrange to have the picture booklet placed on display at an event where members of the parish might appreciate the effort, as well as Jesus' presence in their lives as Living Water. Or, display the booklet as part of a presentation conducted by the group—perhaps directed to younger children or to parents and siblings. The following questions could be included in the presentation: How do you experience Jesus' Living Water? What does Jesus' Living Water mean to you? How do you seek to share this gift with others?

Living Water Scripture Verses

The following verses trace the theme of Living Water from both the Old Testament and the New Testament.

► Genesis 1:1-2; 9-10

► Deuteronomy 8:7-9

► Psalm 1:1-3

► Psalm 23:1-2

► Psalm 41:1-2a

► Psalm 65:9-10

► Isaiah 35:5-7

► Isaiah 41:17-20

► Isaiah 58:11

► Matthew 3:11

► John 4:7-15

► John 7:37-38

► John 13:3-5

► Revelation 7:15-17

Flowing with Justice

<u>Amos 5:24</u>

But let justice roll down like waters,
and righteousness
like an ever-flowing stream.

Learn

Participants will research the themes of justice and righteousness and compile definitions, examples, scripture verses, and personal statements in the form of a litany.

Locate

► Bibles

► Chalk or markers

► Chalkboard, newsprint, or whiteboard

► Paper

► Pencils

► Pens

► Reference materials—books or internet sources

  ► Bible Concordance

  ► Bible Dictionary

  ► Dictionary

  ► Thesaurus

► Tape, masking

Lead

Isaiah, Amos, and other Old Testament books of the Prophets are full of poetic and powerful statements about justice. Amos 5:24 says, "Let justice roll down like waters, and righteousness like an ever-flowing stream." In other places in the Bible a thirst for justice—or fair treatment—is described. During this activity young people will discover definitions of important words related to justice, explore scripture verses that talk about this topic, write their own statements about thirsting for justice, and combine these components to use in a litany on the theme.

As the students arrive, organize them into two teams. One way to do this is to ask everyone who was born between January and June to sit together on one side of the room and everyone with a birthday from July to December to gather on the other side of the space. After the groups are formed, name one the "justice" team and the other the "righteousness" unit. Begin by reading Amos 5:24. Invite the justice team to repeat part of the verse, "Let justice roll down like waters." Tell the righteousness team to respond with the second part of the verse, "And righteousness like an everflowing stream." Repeat the phrases back and forth several times.

Next, tell the groups that they will each spend time considering the meaning of their assigned word including definitions, descriptions, examples, guesses, and phrases. Assign an area for each group to work and direct their attention to the chalkboard and chalk, newsprint and markers, paper and pencils, or whiteboard and markers they are to use.

When the teams run out of ideas, provide each group with research tools in the form of print materials or internet sites. Instruct the participants to look up their word - justice or righteousness—and to record everything they learn about it. Show them how to use any reference materials that might be new to them. Ask the students to try to figure out things like: Why is justice compared to rolling water and righteousness to an ever-flowing stream? What is flowing water like and how can it be described? Make sure that each team member is included in the process and given a task to complete so that some are not sitting on the sidelines while others do all the work. Be available to answer questions and to help the students as needed.

After the research is concluded, tell each team to use the information they gathered to write five statements on their theme. For example, the justice team will write, "Justice is..." and complete the sentence, making five statements about the meaning of justice. The righteousness team will write, "Righteousness is..." and complete five sentences making statements about the meaning of righteousness. Each team will also choose five Bible verses or phrases which they especially like from the list of passages they found in the concordance.

When this part of the project is complete, tell the two groups that they will combine their statements and verses to form a litany.

Explain the pattern:

Justice:	Let justice roll down like waters.
Righteousness:	And righteousness like an ever-flowing stream.
Justice:	Justice is... (Statement 1) (Verse 1)
Justice:	Let justice roll down like waters.
Righteousness:	And righteousness like an ever-flowing stream.
Righteousness:	Righteousness is ... (Statement 1) (Verse 1)
Justice:	Let justice roll down like waters.
Righteousness:	And righteousness like an ever-flowing stream.
Justice:	Justice is... (Statement 2) (Verse 2)

The pattern continues until each team's five statements and five verses have been spoken. End the litany by repeating Amos 5:24 two more times.

Have both groups work together to print the complete litany on a chalkboard, newsprint, or whiteboard. Use a different color of chalk or marker for each group, if possible.

Read the litany together, with each team reciting its statements and verses in turn. Each line can be read by the entire justice or righteousness group, or various parts can be assigned so that each individual or small group reads a part. Be sure that the refrain from Amos is spoken in unison. If there is interest, and time allows, the students could also choose some motions to accompany their readings.

 After the litany, talk about the similarity between justice and righteousness. Explain to the students that in many ways they are all on the same team. Discuss ways in which they can work together to allow justice and righteousness to flow and to bring water to all those who do not experience justice and righteousness.

This activity could be extended by writing the parts of the litany on pages and illustrating them. If the litany turns out well, consider other ways in which it might be used. Give it to a pastor for possible use in a worship service, submit it for publication in the church's newsletter, read it with another class of students, or send copies home for the participants to show and read with their families.

Filling a Cup in Jesus' Name

Mark 9:41

For truly I tell you, whoever gives you a cup of water to drink because you bear the name of Christ will by no means lose the reward.

Learn

Participants will shape a cup out of clay and use it as a reminder of ministering to others in Jesus' name.

Locate

▸ Bible
▸ Clay, self-drying
▸ Cup
▸ Instruments and tools such as craft sticks, flatware, and toothpicks
▸ Knife, blunt
▸ Newspaper
▸ Towels, wet cloth or paper

Advance Preparation

▸ Cut clay into individual pieces, one or two for each participant.
▸ Dampen cloth or paper towels to use for the project.

Lead

In Mark 9:41, Jesus promises a reward to those who bring drink to the thirsty. Jesus' words are a reminder that often we minister to others and are ministered to by others because we are part of the family of Christ. When we bring a drink to the thirsty, we quench a physical need. When we bring an expression of love, we quell a spiritual need. By shaping a cup out of clay, everyone will be reminded of the many ways to serve Jesus by serving others.

Gather in a circle on the floor or around tables. Propose a question to the group: Who are people you know who are in need of a drink of water? Pass a cup around the circle and ask each person, in turn, to tell a way in which it could be used to bring a drink of water to someone in Jesus' name. Each participant should begin with the phrase, "In Jesus' name I could use this cup to ...." Group members may name things such as, "Give my little sister a drink since she can't reach the faucet" or "Bring some water to a friend who just completed a race." Make sure that everyone has an opportunity to share at least one idea with the class.

Next, invite the group to engage in an art project to illustrate this theme. Give each person a few pieces of newspaper to lay on the floor or to place on a table as a work space. Also provide wet cloth or paper towels. Then distribute a piece of clay to each student. Instruct them to get a feel for the clay by molding it in their hands. Tell them they can soften it by working it into different shapes in their palms and fingers. Instruct them to make the clay pliable by shaping it in whatever ways they would like but caution them to refrain from creating an object at this point.

After they have worked with the clay for a little while, ask the students to use it to make something that symbolizes an abundance of water. Tell them to use their imaginations to choose what shapes they will make. One person might form many drops of water while another sculptor may flatten the clay in the shape of a lake. Allow time for the participants to explain their symbols to each other.

Now, ask the participants to change their clay into a shape or a symbol that shows a lack of water. This could be a concrete symbol like a wilting flower. Or, it could also be something which shows a feeling like a person's expression of despair.

Read Mark 9:41 to the participants. Ask the students to use their clay to shape a drinking cup. Encourage them to be creative and to design their cups in any way they like. Provide simple, blunt tools such as craft sticks, flatware, or toothpicks which could be used to make designs, to etch symbols, or to further shape the surface of the clay. When complete, allow more time for the participants to share their work with each other and to explain any special features or meanings of their cups.

Ask the group members to hold their finished cups in their hands. Go around the circle, allowing each person to complete the prayer sentence, "Thank you, God, that I received water in your name when ...." For example, "when we were working hard at church clean-up day and Mr. Pak brought us each a soda." After each person has said thank you to God, continue with prayers of petition. Complete the sentence, Help me to offer a cup of water in your name by .... For instance, helping to serve refreshments at Vacation Bible School this summer.

Before the session ends, discuss ways in which the cups might be used. Inform the participants that the clay cups are not safe for drinking. Instead, the cups will remind them to serve Christ by serving others. The cups could be used to water plants in their home or to hold slips of paper with names of people who need their help and prayers. The cups could be used as banks in which to save change. When collected, the group could give the money to a water-related project. Ask the participants to name other ways in which they might safely use their cups. Before the students leave, instruct them to wrap their cups in damp paper towels to transport them home. Set out at home, the clay will air dry in a few days.

I WAS A STRANGER

In today's culture, the word stranger has developed negative connotations. Generally, it calls to mind someone who is different and, often, someone who could be dangerous. Frequently, our immediate response to a stranger is caution. Parents, rightfully, protect their children from strangers by giving them warnings about associating with unknown people.

In the Bible, the term sojourner more aptly describes the intended meaning of the word stranger. A sojourner is one who travels through or lives in a place which is uncomfortable or unfamiliar to him or her. This person does not have roots in the area or family or friends nearby. Sojourners are dependent on the hospitality of those with whom they come into contact. In many ways all Christians are strangers and sojourners throughout their lives, especially as popular culture becomes increasingly alien to Christian lifestyles and values. Many of the ways in which people became strangers in Bible times will be similar to those explored in the lessons in this chapter.

Fortunately, scripture provides a model for how strangers should be treated. Many of God's special followers were strangers at one time and had to depend on the hospitality of others to exist or even to do their ministry. Throughout the Old Testament, God encourages people to show compassion to strangers. The wandering Israelites were sojourners who moved through the desert or settled among foreign people, depending only on the hospitality of others in God's name to survive. In the Gospels, Jesus often welcomed or was welcomed by strangers. Several New Testament letters, like 1 Timothy 3:2 and Titus 1:8, list hospitality as one of the primary qualities which church leaders should display.

Ten lessons in this chapter offer a variety of suggestions and techniques to explore the theme, "I Was a Stranger." Use them to consider biblical themes such as becoming a stranger, meeting new people, and ministering in Jesus' name.

Chart

Lesson	Scripture	Theme	Activity/Method	Page
Overview	▶ Matthew 25:35c, 38a, 43a, 44a ▶ 1 Timothy 3:2 ▶ Titus 1:8	▶ Stranger		91
Displaying Hospitality	▶ 1 Peter 4:9-10	▶ Symbols of Hospitality ▶ Welcome	▶ Art: Welcome Wreath	94
Welcoming New Neighbors	▶ Romans 12:13	▶ Friendship ▶ Newcomers in the Community, Parish, and School	▶ Art: Pin Punched Paper Heart Decoration	96
Putting Out the Welcome Mat	▶ Acts 16:13-15	▶ Definition/ Examples of Welcome	▶ Art: Graffiti Wall ▶ Creative Writing: Acrostic Poem	100
Talking at Home	▶ Luke 15:11-32	▶ Family Situations	▶ Drama: Improvisation	102
Engaging Others	▶ Genesis 19:1-3	▶ Welcome Customs around the World	▶ Game: World of Welcome Matching Game	105
Singing the Language of Love	▶ Matthew 22:36-40 ▶ 1 John 4:7-11	▶ Love in Various Languages	▶ Art: Love Mobile ▶ Music: "Love In Any Language"	108
Offering a Prayer	▶ Ruth 2	▶ Everyday Events/ Strangers	▶ Art: P-R-A-Y-ing Hands ▶ Creative Writing: Acrostic Poem	111
Showing Kindness to All	▶ Hebrews 13:2	▶ Ministering to Strangers	▶ Photography: Film - *Martin the Cobbler* ▶ Puppetry: Plastic Tub Rod Puppet ▶ Storytelling: Book - *Cobbler Martin* ▶ Storytelling – Story - "Where Love Is, God Is"	113

Blessing a Stranger	▶ Genesis 18:1-10 ▶ Genesis 29:9-20 ▶ 1 Kings 17:8-16 ▶ 2 Kings 4:8-17 ▶ Luke 1:26-38 ▶ Luke 10:25-37 ▶ John 11:17-44 ▶ Acts 16:11-15	▶ Biblical Examples – Hospitality to Strangers	▶ Game: Riddles	115
Making New Friends	▶ Acts 9:26-28 ▶ Acts 11:19-26	▶ Inviting/Making Friends	▶ Dance/Gesture/Movement: Friendship Song ▶ Music: Friendship Song	119

Displaying Hospitality

1 Peter 4:9-10

Be hospitable to one another without complaining. Like good stewards of the manifold grace of God, serve one another with whatever gift each of you has received.

Learn

Participants will remember the biblical principle of hospitality as they create a wreath as a symbol of welcome.

Locate

- ► Bible
- ► Covering for table(s)
- ► Craft sticks or toothpicks
- ► Glue, tacky
- ► Paint, acrylic for wood
- ► Paint brushes
- ► Markers, permanent or paint sticks
- ► Raffia or ribbon, 1/4"
- ► Shirts, smocks, or protective covering for clothing
- ► Wooden "Welcome" cutouts, 1 per wreath, or craft sticks or wooden ice cream spoons
- ► Wreaths, 3" grapevine—1 per participant

Advance Preparation

- ► Cover a table, or as many tables as needed, with paper or plastic.
- ► Pre-cut three pieces of raffia, or ribbon, for each wreath to the following measurements: one yard, four inches, and eight inches.

Lead

In 1 Peter 4:9-10, Christians are told to use their gifts to show hospitality as an expression of love. One way to offer hospitality to others, and even turn strangers into friends, is by inviting people to our homes. While the outside appearance of a home often suggests signs of welcome, the exterior can also make a person feel uncomfortable as they approach a building or a door. Ask the participants to offer examples of things which make a home appear inviting, such as open curtains, an outside light, or a shoveled sidewalk. Encourage the group to share things about their own homes which show that others are welcome there.

Invite the participants to make a sign of welcome, a wreath, which they can display in their homes. Distribute protective wear for each person's clothing such as shirts or smocks. Gather around a table or tables which have been pre-covered with paper or plastic. Pour the paint into containers and set them within the reach of each person for sharing. Provide paint brushes as well.

Give each person a wooden "welcome" cutout. Instruct the artists to paint the cut-outs, covering all surfaces. Set them aside to dry. If using the alternative supplies, paint the entire craft stick or wooden spoon and allow it to dry completely. When dry, provide paint sticks or permanent markers and direct each person to write the word "Welcome" on the wooden piece.

While the paint is drying, make bows out of the pre-cut pieces of raffia or ribbon. Demonstrate how to make a bow by folding the one-yard piece back and forth in three-inch lengths. While holding tightly in the middle, tie the short piece around the center,

securing it with two knots. Glue the bow in place on the top or bottom of the wreath. Use a craft stick or toothpick to liberally spread the tacky glue. Tie the eight-inch piece of raffia through the center, making a knot. This can be used to hang the wreath. Distribute the raffia or ribbon pieces to each person and guide the process of making and attaching the bows.

Finish the decoration by gluing the painted "Welcome" on the top or bottom, opposite the bow. Encourage the learners to display their wreaths in a place at home which will be seen by people who come to their door.

Welcoming New Neighbors

Romans 12:13
Contribute to the needs of the saints;
Extend hospitality to strangers.

Learn

Participants will create pin punched paper heart decorations to give as gifts to newcomers in the community.

Locate

► Bible

► Copy machine or printer

► Hole punch

► Markers or pens, fine-tipped

► Paper for copy machine or printer

► Paper, white drawing or watercolor weight

► Pencils

► Pins, dressmaker-type, nails, or needles

► Resource sheet: "Pattern for Three-inch Hearts"

► Ribbon, string, thread, or yarn

► Scissors

► Towels, wash cloths, or pieces of foam rubber—1 per person

Advance Preparation

► Cut ribbon, string, thread, or yarn into eight-inch lengths. One piece is needed for each completed heart decoration.

► Make copies of the Pattern for Three-inch Heart resource sheet to share with the participants.

Lead

Many people make several moves during their lifetime. According to census data, the average number of moves per person is 11 or 12. When people arrive in a new place they can feel like everyone there already has friends or family, while they are strangers to those around them. Opening one's heart to accept new people can help newcomers feel welcome rather than alone and isolated. In this lesson, the participants will make pin punched paper heart decorations to give as welcome gifts to new people in the community.

Ask the participants if any of them have ever moved—from one apartment or house to another or even to a different city, state, or country. Discuss questions like: What did it feel like to leave familiar friends? What was it like to move to a place where everyone knew each other and you didn't know anyone? How did it feel to make a new friend? How does someone go about making a friend when they are the new person? In addition, invite volunteers to share experiences of befriending a person—child, youth, or adult - who was new to the local community, school, or parish.

Remark that sometimes people are hesitant to make new friends. Often they are satisfied with the friends they have. They might think, I have enough friends; I don't need to make a new one. Or, I don't have time for other people. Some might even feel jealous or scared that his or her current friends might like a new person better than them. Remind the group that when people open their hearts

to include others there is enough friendship to be shared with everyone.

Tell the learners that they will be making pin punched paper hearts to use in welcoming new people to their community, church, or school. Note that these decorations could be hung on door knobs in an apartment building, a senior living complex, or a newly built housing project. They could also be delivered to the doors of new families attending the church or school or moving into the block or neighborhood. Whichever project is chosen, tell the participants about the people who will be receiving the hearts they will make. Imagine what these folks might have felt like leaving their previous homes. If information is available, report the number of new families that have transferred to the school or church in the last few months or year.

To begin the project, place a folded hand towel, dish towel, wash cloth, or a piece

of foam rubber at each place. Distribute drawing or watercolor paper, pencils, patterns for hearts, and scissors to the students. Instruct the artists to use a pencil to trace the heart pattern very lightly on a piece of paper and to use a scissors to cut out the shape. It is important not to make a fold in the paper as a fold will mar the appearance of this project. Allow the students to cut out as many hearts as time allows.

Explain that the heart decorations are made by poking a pin, needle, or nail in and out of a piece of paper to create a design. Tell the learners to place a heart on the foam rubber or the towel in front of them. Instruct them to hold the heart steady with one hand and to use a pin, needle, or nail in the other hand to lightly poke holes through the paper. Direct them to make holes around the edges of the heart and to create a design in the center of the shape as well. Encourage creativity by noting that various textures can be achieved by using different sized implements for the project. Vary the size of the holes by poking the point part way or all the way through the paper. However, warn the workers not to place their hands too heavily on the heart or the surface will become bent and the designs will not show up.

When the decorations are completed, punch a hole in the top of each heart. Loop a piece of ribbon, string, thread, or yarn through the hole to serve as a hanger for the ornament.

Allow the participants to make as many hearts as time allows. If creating multiple hearts, suggest that they make one to take home to hang in their rooms to remind them to be friendly to new people. When the hearts are completed, simple messages can be written on them. Use fine point pens or permanent markers to print cheerful messages such as,

▶ Welcome! Hope you enjoy your new home!

or

▶ Welcome to _____ (fill in the name of the parish, school, or town).

Remind the participants about the people who will receive the hearts and how the decorations will be distributed. If a field trip to an apartment complex or a senior center can be arranged, distribute them as a group. As an alternative, take a few volunteers at a time to various places on pre-determined dates.

End the time together by instructing the students to pick up a heart and to stand in a circle. After the circle is formed ask everyone to take one or two steps back. Tell the students to look at the spaces which have been created on each side of them. Point out that there is plenty of room in the circle to add more friends. Close with prayer for the people who will receive the hearts. Explain that the leader will begin the prayer with a sentence or two and then the participants, in turn, can say one word, phrase, or sentence asking God to be with those in need of hospitality and welcome. The leader, or another adult, can add a simple conclusion to the prayer. After the prayer, collect the hearts which will be distributed at a later time and remind the students to take home any hearts that they have made for that purpose.

Pattern for Three-Inch Hearts

Putting Out the Welcome Mat

Acts 16:15

When she [Lydia] and her household were baptized, she urged us, saying, 'If you have judged me to be faithful to the Lord, come and stay at my home.'

Learn

Participants will explore the meaning of the word welcome by composing an acrostic poem and creating a graffiti wall.

Locate

► Bible
► Catalogs or magazines
► Crayons or markers
► Dictionary
► Glue
► Paper such as butcher, newsprint, or tablecloth
► Tape, duct or masking
► Scissors

Advance Preparation

► Cover a door of the classroom with paper. Depending on the size of the group, one or both sides of the door may be used for the project.
► Print the word W E L C O M E vertically down the center of the paper.

Lead

Everyone experiences being a stranger at sometime. This may happen to people on the first day of school, when moving to a different neighborhood, while attending camp, on a vacation, or at a new activity. During this lesson a door of the classroom will be turned into a graffiti wall and provide a way for everyone to work together to explore the theme of offering welcome to others.

As the learners arrive, create a spirit of welcome by inviting everyone to gather around the paper-covered door. Take time to greet each person by name and encourage all of the participants to welcome each other as well. After everyone has assembled, call

attention to the word that has been printed on the paper. Ask the students to suggest definitions of the word welcome. Then use a dictionary to look up its meaning. Talk about places where individuals in the group have felt welcome and about situations when they did not feel welcome. Places of welcome could be at a relative's home, a neighborhood picnic, or a school function. Situations when people felt unwelcome might be in a group where there is a clique, at an upscale restaurant, or at an event in a different city. Allow everyone to share one example for each question.

Tell the participants that they are going to use the paper-covered door to create a graffiti wall of drawings and writings and to compose an acrostic poem to convey things people can do to help others feel welcome.

Begin by composing an acrostic poem. Explain that for each letter of the word welcome, a word or a phrase that begins with that letter and fits the theme is written on that line. Offer examples of welcome words such as W- wave, L - laugh, M - meet.

Provide crayons or markers and take turns writing words on the paper. Depending on the age of the participants, people may print their own words and phrases directly on the door or younger children may suggest words to a leader who can write them on the door.

Continue by turning the door into a graffiti wall. Suggest that the students draw pictures and add words related to the theme of welcome anywhere on the paper. Ideas could include giving a high five, eating lunch with someone, and playing a game. If desired, pictures which demonstrate ways in which people make others feel welcome may be cut from catalogs and magazines and glued or taped to the door.

When the group has finished, review the comments together and add any others which the group may suggest. If time permits read Acts 16:13-15, the New Testament Bible story of Lydia, a new believer who showed welcome to Paul during his ministry. Encourage the artists and writers to share the graffiti wall with parents, friends, or other classes in the next few days or weeks.

Talking at Home

Luke 15:32
But we had to celebrate and rejoice, because this brother of yours was dead and has come to life; he was lost and has been found.

Learn

Participants will act out scenarios that emphasize positive relationships between people living in the same household.

Locate

► Bag, basket, or other container
► Bible
► Copy machine or printer
► Paper for copy machine or printer
► Paper cutter or scissors
► Resource sheet: "Family Situations"

Advance Preparation

► Duplicate a copy of the Family Situations resource sheet.
► Cut the duplicated sheet into individual scenarios and place the separated pieces in a bag, basket, or other container.

Lead

Sometimes people living in the same household become strangers to each other. When brothers and sisters, fathers and mothers, family and friends residing in the same home do not have or take time to spend together they can become isolated from each other. Because of this, conflicts may arise due to lack of communication. In this lesson, participants will act out ways of dealing with a variety of family situations and discuss suggestions to stay close to people in their living environment.

Begin the lesson by reading the story of the Prodigal Son, found in Luke 15:11-32. If time allows, assign or choose parts including Jesus as the narrator, the older son, the father, the younger son, plus others in the household or village, and act out the story with the group. After the drama, take time to comment on each character in the story and ask questions such as: What caused the relationships to become strained? How were the broken relationships repaired? Provide an opportunity for volunteers to share their ideas.

Next, focus the discussion on contemporary family life. Explain the importance of caring about others feelings and needs, not just our own. When we stop paying attention to the likes and dislikes or the activities and interests of family members, these important people can become like strangers to us.

Tell the learners that they will be acting out family situations that might cause people to become strangers to each other. Offer an example of a scenario such as:

Oliver is with a group of friends when he says, "My family is like a bunch of strangers all living in the same house. We never see each other or do anything together!" Act out suggestions to respond to Oliver's comment.

Invite volunteers to offer responses to Oliver's situation—verbally and dramatically. Suggestions might include: plan a family meal and take time to talk about each person's day; go for ice cream and spend time catching up on each other's plans; double up on family responsibilities such as cleaning, cooking, or yard work and listen to each other's stories while working together.

Organize the class into groups of two or three participants. Invite a representative from each group to choose a piece of paper from the container and read it to the others on the team. Allow time for each duo or trio to prepare an improvised drama for their situation. Then, have the actors take turns presenting their scenes to the entire class.

After each presentation, ask volunteers to add comments, ideas, or solutions on the scenario. Allow the participants the opportunity to talk about how the situations relate to their own family experiences, however direct the conversation away from personal or sensitive topics.

Conclude the class by offering a prayer asking for God's help in maintaining positive relationships in family situations.

Family Situations

- Andrew and his family use dinner time to keep from becoming strangers. Show what they do.

- Anika and her brother do so many separate activities and spend so much time at friends' houses that they are hardly ever home. Show what happens to their family relationships. Then show what they can do about it.

- Austin, his brothers, and his parents each go to different activities every day of the week. Show how they might start to treat each other negatively and how they can work together as a family to get everything done.

- Brianna's family is home for a holiday but everyone is doing his or her own separate activities. Show how they can spend time together and grow as a family instead.

- Nathan had a fight with his sister. He hasn't talked to her in two weeks. Show what he could do to bridge the gap.

- Raj's mother works very hard. He feels like he doesn't get to see her enough. She also feels sad, but has to work. Show what they can do to talk about this and to feel close to each other.

- Shawnee's family asks each other questions that help them stay informed about and interested in each other's lives. For example, "How was work today?" or "What was your favorite part of the movie?" Show how they do it.

- Cindy's father lives in another town. She only gets to see him every other weekend. Show how she can stay close to him so that they do not become strangers.

- Troy's older brother is home from college for the summer. They have not seen much of each other during the year. Act out ways they can do things together and get to know each other again during these months.

Engaging Others

Genesis 19:1

The two angels came to Sodom in the evening, and Lot was sitting in the gateway of Sodom. When Lot saw them, he rose to meet them, and bowed down with his face to the ground.

Learn

Participants will learn about welcome customs around the world by playing a hospitality matching game.

Locate

- ► Bible
- ► Copy machine or printer
- ► Paper for copy machine or printer
- ► Pencils or pens
- ► Resource materials on welcome customs in various countries
- ► Resource sheet: "World of Welcome Matching Game"

Advance Preparation

- ► Duplicate one copy of the World of Welcome Matching Game resource sheet for each participant.

Lead

Many countries of the world have their own traditions of expressing hospitality and welcome to guests and visitors. Some of these customs may seem strange to people who have not experienced them before or have not grown up with them. During this lesson, the participants will play a matching game to explore some of these practices and they will learn about people who are different from them.

Invite volunteers to name ways in which they are welcomed when they visit a relative's home, go to a store, or attend an event. Responses might include a family member gives a hug, someone says hello, or an usher shows them to a seat. Ask if anyone has ever been welcomed with a necklace of flowers, a plate of bread and salt, or a spray of perfume. Tell the group that countries throughout the world have unique traditions of welcome. Invite them to play a World of Welcome Matching Game to learn more about customs of hospitality throughout the world.

Distribute a game sheet and a pencil or a pen to each person. Explain that each statement on the left side of the paper describes a greeting practice in a certain country. Read through the list. Tell the group that the goal is to match the statement on the left with the word on the right which names the item used to express hospitality. To make a match, use the pencil or pen to connect the sentence and the word with a line. Provide time for the students to work on the answers. When the game is completed, invite the learners to share their answers. The answers are:

1. D
2. H
3. B
4. F
5. A
6. G
7. C
8. E

Ask the group to name additional customs of welcome they have experienced or of which they are aware.

As an additional or an alternate way to play the game, distribute one statement or answer to each person and instruct the pairs to find each other.

Conclude the lesson by reading Genesis 19:1-3, the story of Lot welcoming strangers with food and lodging. Challenge the participants to be willing to accept hospitality from and to provide welcome for others in many ways.

World of Welcome Matching Game

Match a custom of hospitality with a place where it is practiced.

Places

1. In Somalia guests entering a home are sprayed with sweet smelling _____.

2. Beautiful floral necklaces given to newcomers in Hawaii are called _____.

3. After eating a good meal in a Turkish home, a guest may show appreciation with a loud _____.

4. Traditional welcoming ceremonies in Russia involve breaking bread and dipping it into _____.

5. Hospitality in French homes is shown by offering visitors a selection of candies and _____.

6. When family, friends or strangers arrive at a home in the United States, the host or hostess welcomes the guests by offering to take their _____.

7. In England the fruit that has become a symbol of hospitality is the _____.

8. "Welkommen," the German word for welcome is displayed in homes, stores, and public places on _____.

Customs

A. Chocolates

B. Burp

C. Pineapple

D. Perfume

E. Signs

F. Salt

G. Coats

H. Leis

Singing the Language of Love

1 John 4:7

Beloved, let us love one another, because love is from God; everyone who loves is born of God and knows God.

Learn

Participants will express love in many languages by constructing a mobile and singing a song.

Locate

- Bible
- Copy machine or printer
- Glue
- Guitar or keyboard
- Hangers
- Hole punch
- Magazines
- Markers
- Music for "Love in Any Language" by Jon Mohr and John Mays
- Paper for copy machine or printer
- Poster board
- Resource sheet: "Many Ways to Say Love"
- Ribbon or yarn
- Scissors

Advance Preparation

- Arrange for a musician to accompany the singing on a guitar or a keyboard.
- Learn the American Sign Language (ASL) motions for key words in the song "Love in Any Language" using an internet site such as Handspeak.com or SigningSavvy.com or a phone app with sign language instructions and visuals. Focus on the following words: love, language, heart, pulls, together, apart, world, spoken, here.
- Make a copy of the "Many Ways to Say Love" resource sheet for each participant.

Lead

Jesus' message can be summarized in one word: love. In Matthew 22:36-40 Jesus tells his followers to love God with all their hearts and to love their neighbors as themselves. Neighbors include people who live across the street as well as those who reside around the world. Neighbors may be family and friends, casual acquaintances or total strangers, as well as classmates and team members. Regardless of the relationship, in 1 John 4:7 Jesus commands people to love each other: "Let us love one another, for love comes from God."

In countries throughout the world, the word for love is expressed in many languages: *amor* in French, *liebe* in German, and *szeretet* in Hungarian. Help the participants realize the importance of showing love for all of God's people by teaching them the song "Love in Any Language." The chorus is especially easy to learn and the verses may be sung by the entire group or by individuals who would like to share a solo. Play or sing the song for the listeners. Then teach it to the learners and sing it as a group.

Once the words and tune have been mastered, add sign language to the song to help the pupils interpret and express the meaning of the key words, especially the lines of the chorus. Refer the participants to an internet source or a phone app on American Sign Language if helpful. Practice the signs for the chorus and then combine them with the words and the music of the song.

Add another dimension to the lesson by making love mobiles as an individual or group project. Tell the class that they will be writing the word love in various languages and finding pictures of people and places to paste on poster board shapes which will be attached to the mobile. Supply the resource sheet that lists the word love written in many different languages. Try pronouncing some of the words together.

As an individual project, invite each artist to select several countries to illustrate on his or her mobile. Distribute poster board, scissors, and markers. Tell the pupils to cut four to six shapes from the heavy paper. Instruct them to write love in a different language on each piece. Provide magazines and have the learners find pictures of people and places from the countries represented by their words. After cutting them out, offer glue to attach the photos to the back side of each poster board shape. Provide hole punches, string or yarn, and clothes hangers. Help the participants punch a hole at the top of each shape and cut a length of ribbon or yarn to string through it. Tie the pieces to a hanger.

For a group activity, begin with a large form, such as a hula hoop. Invite each participant to choose one country to illustrate with a love word and interesting pictures. Tie the completed pieces to the mobile. Display the completed project in a place where many people will see it.

Conclude the lesson by singing and signing the song, "Love in Any Language." If time and interest permit, additional or alternate songs to use with this activity include "Jesu, Jesu, Fill Us with Your Love," a melody from Ghana with words by Tom Colvin, and "They'll Know We Are Christian by Our Love" by Peter Scholtes.

Challenge the group to use the art they created and the music they learned to help expand their outlook on the countless number of people in the world—and near to home—to whom they can show love in many ways.

Many Ways to Say Love

Czech	laska	laz-kah
Danish	kaerlighed	care-lah-did
Dutch	liefde	leaf-duh
English	love	luh-vuh
Finnish	rakkaus	rak-ouse
French	l'amour	la-more
German	liebe	lee-buh
Greek	agape	ah-gah-pee
Hungarian	szerelem	seh-reh-lem
Irish	gra	grah
Italian	amore	a-more-eh
Latin	amor	ah-more
Norwegian	kjaerlighet	seh-reh-lem
Polish	milosc	me-low-sich
Portuguese	amor	ah-moor
Spanish	amor	ah-more
Swahili	upendo	oo-pend-doh
Swedish	karlek	shar-lay-ek

Offering a Prayer

Ruth 2:10

Then she fell prostrate, with her face to the ground, and said to him, 'Why have I found favor in your sight, that you should take notice of me, when I am a foreigner'?

Learn

Participants will discover everyday ways children, youth, and adults become strangers and create P-R-A-Y-ing hands as a reminder to help these people.

Locate

- Bible
- Bulletins and newsletters from churches and schools
- Chalk
- Chalkboard, newsprint, or whiteboard
- Hole Punch
- Magazines
- Markers
- Metal rings or paper clips
- Newspaper
- Paper, construction
- Scissors

Lead

People become strangers in many different ways. Some of them are planned, or intentional, like going to a different city on a trip or attending a sporting event in a large stadium. Some are unexpected, or unintentional, such as being involved in an accident on an isolated road or being stranded away from home in a storm. In this lesson, participants will learn some of the ways in which people become strangers and discover how they can extend a hand of concern in many of these situations.

Begin the lesson by sharing the Old Testament Bible story of Ruth. Ruth became a stranger when she journeyed to a new land with her mother-in-law, Naomi, after the death of their husbands. When Ruth searched for food in the field, she was extended kindness by the owner of the land, Boaz, who invited her to glean grain for her family.

Next, show the group bulletin, magazine, and newspaper photographs and stories that illustrate the theme of becoming a stranger. Invite the participants to share experiences which they or people they know have had in this connection. Brainstorm and record a list of many of the ways this occurs, such as:

- Accident
- Automobile break-down
- Business trip
- Church camp
- College
- Earthquake

- ▶ Fire
- ▶ Foreign Exchange Student
- ▶ Hurricane
- ▶ Military service
- ▶ Missions
- ▶ Moving
- ▶ Stranded
- ▶ Tornado
- ▶ Vacation
- ▶ Work camp

Regardless of the ways in which people become strangers, they need to experience God's love. One way for the learners to become involved in offering care and concern is by using their hands. They can contribute money to a disaster relief offering, make cookies to send to college students or military personnel, or volunteer their time and talent to repair a home. Another way is to fold or raise their hands in prayer. Lead the group in an activity that will help them remember people who have become strangers through various circumstances. Help the pupils create a unique prayer chain to reach out to people near and far.

Place construction paper, scissors, and markers within sharing distance of the students. Direct each person to choose a piece of paper and to trace his or her hand onto it. Tell the artists to cut out the tracings. Using markers, have each person write his or her name on the shape. Invite the group members to choose a situation or a specific person to remember in prayer. The prayer requests should be written on the hands, as well as verbalized. Another activity would be to instruct everyone to write, in order, the letters of the word P-R-A-Y on the tops of the fingers. Ask the participants to think of words, beginning with each of these letters, which describe how they can reach out to strangers. More specifically, help the learners identify ways and words to illustrate how their hands can be used to show strangers God's love. For example, P - pray, R - repair, A - allowance, Y - yard work. These words may be written on the fingers or just recited and remembered.

When the hands have been completed, punch a hole in the top and bottom of each shape. Gather the group in a circle and invite each person, in turn, to offer his or her prayer. Link all of the hands together to form a prayer chain by connecting them with metal rings or paper clips. Hang the prayer chain in the classroom and invite the learners to remember these strangers in their prayers during class time and throughout the week.

Showing Kindness to All

Hebrews 13:2

Do not neglect to show hospitality to strangers, for by doing that some have entertained angels without knowing it.

Learn

Participants will review the story of Martin the Cobbler and create rod puppets to tell this tale.

Locate

- ▶ Bible
- ▶ Book – *Cobbler Martin* (Tolstoy, Leo and Bernadette Watts, Illustrator. New York, NY: NorthSouth Books, 2018.)
- ▶ Carpet pad, polyfoam
- ▶ Chopsticks or dowel rods
- ▶ Cotton, fake fur, or yarn
- ▶ Equipment to show film
- ▶ Fabric
- ▶ Felt
- ▶ Film – *Martin the Cobbler* [Many versions available on YouTube.com]
- ▶ Glue, tacky
- ▶ Knife, exacto
- ▶ Needles
- ▶ Pantyhose
- ▶ Plastic tubs from margarine or whipped topping
- ▶ Scissors
- ▶ Story - "Where Love Is, God Is"
- ▶ Styrofoam balls, 3"-5" diameter
- ▶ Thread
- ▶ Trims

Lead

Countless passages in the New Testament, as well as throughout the Bible, make the point that ministering to strangers is actually showing love to Jesus. Leo Tolstoy's short story, "Where Love Is, God Is," adapted into the classic account, Martin the Cobbler, illustrates this theme. During this lesson, share the story by reading a book, showing a film, or telling the tale. Then create puppets to use to share the message with others.

Explain that in Tolstoy's story, Martin, an old cobbler, has lost his family and all interest in living. One night in a dream he is inspired by a voice, which he believes is the Lord's, promising to visit him the next day. By evening his special guest has not arrived, even though several needy people have come to his door and sought and received his aid. That night as Martin reads the scriptures a vision reveals to him that in caring for others he has met Jesus. Renewed and joyful again, Martin joins his old friends in celebrating the winter festival.

Show a film version of the story or read the book, *Cobbler Martin*, to the class to review the tale and to reinforce the message.

Invite the group to make and use puppets to tell this important and inspiring story to others. Review the characters which need to be made including Martin the Cobbler, the three strangers who visit him, and the townspeople.

Explain that the body parts of the puppets are made from several recyclable objects. A Styrofoam ball forms the head, pantyhose becomes the skin, and a plastic margarine or frozen whipping cream tub serves as the shoulders. Strips of carpet pad turn into two arms and a chop stick or dowel rod becomes the handle by which the puppet is operated.

Assign characters to make or have each person or small group select the people they wish to portray. Demonstrate the process to put the pieces of each puppet together.

Insert the stick into the bottom of the Styrofoam ball. After the hole is made, remove the stick. Spread glue on both pieces and re-insert the rod. Allow it to dry. Cut a small hole into the bottom of the plastic tub. Also cut a small slit on each side of the container. Cut arms from the polyfoam carpet pad and fit one into each side slit. Cut a six inch length of pantyhose. Tie off one of the loose ends, pull the material over the ball, and tie the piece around the stick with a strip of yarn. Using felt scraps, cut out eyes, nose, and mouth. Glue them to the head. Choose yarn or fake fur to make hair. If yarn is used, wrap it around the hand or a piece of cardboard several times. Snip open the ends, or leave them looped. Glue or sew the hair to the top of the head. Insert the rod into the hole in the top of the plastic container. Pull the pantyhose through the hole, and tape it to the stick. Place a large piece of tape under the plastic carton to hold up the container. Choose fabric for the costume. Cut a hole into the center of it, and slide it over the puppet's head. Sew the material tightly around the neck. Make a few stitches on each side of the piece underneath the puppet's arms. Add trims to complete the costume. Insert the other chop stick or another piece of dowel rod into one of the puppet's hands. To operate the character, hold the rod under the costume in one hand, and work the rod on the arm with the other hand.

Take time to make the puppets, offering assistance and encouragement as needed.

After the puppets are completed, practice the play, and perform it for other classes, the entire parish, and community groups.

Blessing a Stranger

Genesis 18:2

He looked up and saw three men standing near him. When he saw them, he ran from the tent entrance to meet them, and bowed down to the ground.

Learn

Participants will explore the theme of showing hospitality to strangers as they solve Bible story riddles.

Locate

► Bibles
► Copy machine or printer
► Paper for copy machine or printer
► Pencils or pens
► Resource sheet: "Scripture Riddles"

Advance Preparation

► Duplicate a copy of the Scripture Riddles resource sheet for each participant.

Lead

There are many stories in the Bible of people who welcomed strangers and provided for their needs. In these examples, not only did the sojourners benefit from the kindly actions, God also blessed the person who was willing to be helpful. Though these people did not offer an act of kindness to receive a blessing, God did something special for them all the same. By looking up scripture passages and solving riddles the participants will uncover more about biblical people who shared and received God's blessings by helping others.

Distribute a copy of the Scripture Riddles resource sheet to each person or small group. Explain that they are to read the riddle and guess the person or people who showed hospitality to strangers and to write the name(s) on the line. Next, they are to look up the verses, read the passage, and determine if the answer is correct. After both steps are completed for all of the riddles, check and discuss the passages and the right answers with the entire group.

Answers:

1. Abraham and Sarah
2. Rachel
3. A Widow and her son
4. Shunammite woman
5. Mary and Joseph
6. Martha, Mary, and Lazarus
7. The Good Samaritan
8. Lydia

While discussing the blessings which were received by the welcoming person, make sure to emphasize that receiving a blessing is not the reason for helping someone else.

Encourage the students to welcome others because it is what God wants them to do. However, in doing so we often gain from the experience in many different ways. For instance, when we befriend someone new at school, we also enjoy the fun of having another friend. When we reach out to someone in need, we have the good feeling that comes from caring about other people. Ask the students to share stories of times when they have benefited by acting in caring ways toward someone else.

Conclude the session by offering a prayer asking for God's help in being the blessing in the lives of family, friends, and strangers.

Scripture Riddles

1. These two special people walked out of their tent,
down the road they saw strangers - angels God had sent.
They welcomed them giving them water, food, and rest.
Too old to become parents, with a miracle baby they were blessed.

Guess: _____

Read: Genesis 18:1-10

Answer: _____

≈

2. Tired and thirsty, Jacob spotted a well.
A woman drew him water and let him rest for a spell.
Then she invited him home, into her family's life.
Later both were blessed when she became his wife.

Guess: _____

Read: Genesis 29:9-20

Answer: _____

≈

3. Elijah needed food and a place to stay,
but these two people had only enough for one day.
With the love of the Lord, they opened their door,
and day after day their supplies were restored.

Guess: _____

Read: 1 Kings 17:8-16

Answer: _____

≈

4. This woman saw a holy man named Elisha passing one day.
She and her husband gave him food and built a room for him to stay.
Elisha asked how he could thank her for all that she had done.
God answered Elisha's prayer for her and sent a son.

Guess: _____

Read: 2 Kings 4:8-17

Answer: _____

5. Soon to be married; happy, young, and free,
this couple discovered God would send a stranger - a baby!
The young woman responded, "May God be adored!"
They became the earthly parents of Christ Jesus, our Lord.

Guess _____

Read: Luke 1:26-38

Answer _____

∽

6. These two sisters and a brother made Jesus Christ their friend.
Soon they also welcomed the disciples, time together they would spend.
They were blessed by Jesus' caring and his never-ending love,
and when the brother sadly died, Christ sent a miracle from above.

Guess _____

Read: John 11:17-44

Answer _____

∽

7. Traveling down a lonely road to Jericho,
this man found a foreign stranger laying on the road.
Others passed by and left him bleeding there.
To this day this man is an example of how to care.

Guess _____

Read: Luke 10:25-37

Answer _____

∽

8. Down by the river, this woman knelt and prayed.
God answered her pleas and sent Paul her way.
He told her about Jesus and she felt so blessed.
She invited him to her home to share the happiness.

Guess _____

Read: Acts 16:11-15

Answer _____

Making New Friends

Acts 9:27-28

But Barnabas took him, brought him to the apostles, and described for them how on the road he had seen the Lord, who had spoken to him, and how in Damascus he had spoken boldly in the name of Jesus.

Learn

Participants will use movement and music to the "Friendship Song" to encourage people to welcome others.

Locate

- ▶ Copy machine or printer
- ▶ Music to "Three Blind Mice"
- ▶ Paper for copy machine or printer
- ▶ Resource sheet: "Friendship Song"

Advance Preparation

- ▶ Make copies of "Friendship Song" for the leaders.

Lead

Acts 9 records the story of the change of name and the change of heart of Saul, a man who persecuted followers of Jesus, to Paul, a missionary who invited individuals to become part of Christ's church. Acts 11 also offers an account of Barnabas, Paul's companion, encouraging people to welcome the converted Paul into their midst and to listen to his message. Read portions of these passages, or review the stories, emphasizing the theme of welcome.

Invite the participants to use movement and music to explore the message of invitation and inclusion.

Arrange the group into circles of six or fewer participants. If there are less than six people in each group, be sure that the number sung in the last verse of the song corresponds with the appropriate number of players. Sing or hum the tune to the song "Three Blind Mice" to be sure everyone is familiar with it. Refer to the words of the "Friendship Song." Note that the lyrics are sung to the tune "Three Blind Mice." Invite a leader to begin singing verse one and walking around the circle. At the phrase "Come with me," the leader chooses one person to join with him or her. Continue singing, adding people at the appropriate point in each verse. By picking the next person in the circle the chooser will not hesitate and no one will fear being excluded or left out.

Repeat the entire song several times, giving everyone an opportunity to be the leader or to be near the beginning of the process. For variety, add an action such as skipping, hopping, twirling, or trotting for each verse while walking around the circle.

If possible, arrange for the group to lead younger children, kindergarten through grade three, in the activity. Share the movement and music with family and friends.

Friendship Song

[Tune: Three Blind Mice]

I am one. I am one.

I'm having fun. I'm having fun.

Now let's see what we can do,

come with me and we'll make it two.

We are two. We are two.

We are two. We are two.

Look what we can do.
Look what we can do.

Come with us and you can see

we can turn two into three.

We are three. We are three.

We are three. We are three.

Happy as can be. Happy as can be.

Come with us and make one more

so we'll have a group of four.

We are four. We are four.

We are four. We are four.

Let's add more. Let's add more.

Come with us and make it five.

Celebrate that we're alive.

We are five. We are five.

We are five. We are five.

Glad to be alive. Glad to be alive.

Come with us and we'll all mix.

Now we have a group of six.

We are six. We are six.

Conclusion

Come along. Come along.

Sing our song. Sing our song.

When you reach out to make a friend

you'll be happy in the end.

We are friends. We are friends.

I WAS POOR

Poverty—the lack of sufficient clothing, education, food, medicine, and shelter—is never far from view. Homeless people are seen on the streets of most cities. In rural as well as urban areas, the poor suffer in insufficient and unsafe dwellings. Throughout the world, children are born, live their entire lives, and die without having the basic elements most people consider essential for their existence.

In John 12:8a Jesus said, 'You will always have the poor with you.' The poor, or naked, are referred to many times in the Bible. Old Testament stories include Boaz and Ruth (Ruth 2), Elisha and the Widow's Oil (1 Kings 4:1-7), and Elijah and the woman of Zarephath (1 Kings 17:7-16). For Jesus, helping the poor was a justice issue. Fortunately, Jesus did not just point out the poor and the conditions of poverty, he also gave his disciples instructions for caring for their material needs. For example, in Matthew 25:36, Jesus said 'I was naked and you gave me clothing.' When we care for the physical needs of the poor or needy we are doing it for Jesus.

Because people can be poor in many different ways, the needs of the poor in spirit, those who are sad, discouraged, or lonely, will also be addressed. In Matthew 5:3, the first beatitude listed in the Sermon on the Mount, Jesus said, 'Blessed are the poor in spirit, for theirs is the kingdom of God.' It could also be said, "Blessed are those who see the poor in spirit, for they shall see the kingdom of God."

The ten lessons in this chapter, I Was Poor, will help the participants discover ways of helping the needy, provide opportunities to make a difference, and encourage habits that should continue for a lifetime. In addition, learners will be helped to see and respond to the poor in spirit and, thus, bring the fullness of God's kingdom one step closer to realization.

Chart

Title	Scripture	Theme	Activity/Method	Page
Overview	► Ruth 2 ► 1 Kings 4:1-7 ► 1 Kings 17:7-16 ► Matthew 5:3 ► Matthew 25:36a, 38b, 43b, 44b ► John 12:8a	► Poor		121
Clothing the Poor	► Acts 9:36-41	► Clothing Ministries	► Banners/Textiles: Rag Doll	123
Expressing the Pain	► Psalm 1 – Psalm 7 ► Psalm 25	► Suffering	► Creative Writing: Poems of Lament	125
Becoming Personally Involved	► Acts 6:5	► Personal Commitment	► Drama: Monologues ► Storytelling: First Person Stories	127
Searching for Support	► James 2:14-17	► Support Systems	► Game: Scavenger Hunt	130
Encouraging through Music	► Matthew 25 ► 1 Thessalonians 5:11	► Self Esteem/ Image	► Music: Listen to Lyrics	133
Addressing Unemployment	► Psalm 90:17	► Unemployment	► Art: Woven Mat	135
Giving for the Poor	► Mark 12:41-44	► Coin Projects	► Puppetry: Bottle Rod Puppet	138
Celebrating the Caring	► Luke 6:30-31	► Martinmas Celebration	► Culinary: Cupcakes	141
Responding to Needs	► Romans 15:25, 26	► Unexpected Poverty	► Banners/Textiles: Patchwork Banner or Quilt	143
Helping the Homeless	► Isaiah 58:7	► Homelessness	► Art: Cartoons ► Storytelling: Book – *Benjamin Brody's Backyard Bag*	145

Seeing Jesus

Clothing the Poor

Acts 9:39
All the widows stood beside him, weeping and showing tunics and other clothing that Dorcas had made while she was with them.

Learn

Participants will review the New Testament story of Dorcas, learn about used clothing projects in the community, and create rag dolls as reminders of these ministries.

Locate

- ► Chalk or marker
- ► Chalkboard or newsprint
- ► Embroidery floss and needles, fabric paints, paint markers, or puff paints (optional)
- ► Fiberfill
- ► Glue (optional)
- ► Muslin or other off-white or white material which does not ravel easily - 10" square per person
- ► Needles
- ► Ribbon, 1/8" satin
- ► Roses, small satin (optional)
- ► Scissors

Advance Preparation

- ► Cut fabric into 10" squares.
- ► Cut ribbon into 10" lengths.
- ► Research local and regional agencies that assist in clothing distribution.

Lead

Dorcas, also known as Tabitha, was a disciple in the early church. According to the Acts of the Apostles, she made and repaired clothing to give to the poor, especially widows and orphans. The way Dorcas chose to reach out to others in Jesus' name is an on-going ministry and one in which most people can participate. The reuse of clothing is not only a service to the poor, but also a means of being good stewards of the earth's resources. In this activity, the learners will hear about Dorcas' service to the those in need. They will also discover how clothing ministries continue in their own community and congregation, and create rag dolls to reinforce that clothing can be used over and over in many ways.

Read or summarize the story of Dorcas from Acts 9:36-41. Ask the participants to think of clothing ministries that are available in their own community. Make a list of places they name on a chalkboard or newsprint. Examples include Goodwill Industries, The Salvation Army, St. Vincent de Paul Society, homeless centers, second hand stores, shelters, and thrift shops. Ask the group to tell what they do with their used clothing and if their families have ever donated to one of these groups. Inform the class that any clothing can be reused in some way. Charities that collect clothing distribute or sell the wearable goods to people who need it. Worn out clothes are sold to manufacturing companies who turn them into rag stuffing for toys and other items. The money the organizations receive for the goods is used for various ministries to the poor.

Discuss the ways the congregation participates in clothing the poor. Many churches collect clothes for a mission group in their community or in another area of the country or world, coats to distribute to the homeless in the city, clothes to sell at a rummage sale for missions, or clothing for a family who has lost their belongings in a fire. Also talk about good sources for low cost clothing, instead of always buying new clothes. Hand-me-downs, garage sales, and thrift shops are examples.

Tell the students that in colonial times fabric and other resources were scarce and worn out clothing was used to make rag or handkerchief dolls. Variations of rag dolls have been made in many different places, where people learn to carefully use every resource they have available. Invite the learners to make a simple rag doll to better understand how clothing materials can be recycled.

For the project itself, assign the students a work space at a table. Give a ten-inch square piece of muslin, or other white or off-white fabric, to each participant. Instruct them to lay the fabric in front of them in a shape like a diamond, with a point towards themselves. Distribute a small amount of fiberfill to each person. Tell them to make the head by taking the point farthest away, placing a small amount of stuffing into that corner, and gathering the fabric around it. Tie in place using the thin ribbon. Make a double knot and finish with the long ends of the ribbon hanging down the remaining

portion of the fabric. Tie a bow. Glue a satin rose to the center of the bow, if desired. Pause and help the participants with these steps before proceeding.

Form the hands of the doll in one of two ways. Take the side points of the square and tie each in a small knot. Or, gather the points and tie them in place with a piece of thin ribbon. Make a double knot. Explain that the faces were traditionally left blank.

At this point the doll is finished. However, further decorations are possible if time and interest allows. Provide embroidery floss and needles. Invite the creators to sew a simple running stitch along the lower edge of the "dress." Puff paints, fabric paints, or paint markers could also be used to make a decorative border.

Remind the participants that these rag dolls are one way that clothing materials can be reused. If desired, the group could sell their finished projects to members of the congregation and donate the funds they receive to agencies that work to meet the needs of the poor.

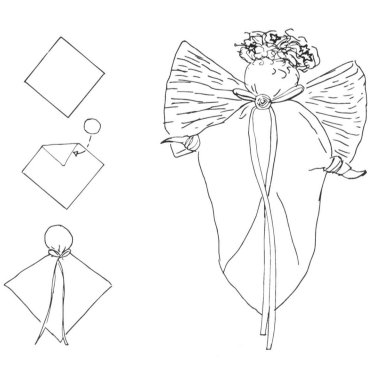

Expressing the Pain

Psalm 25:16
Turn to me and be gracious to me,
for I am lonely and afflicted.

Learn

Participants will read psalms of lament and write poems related to these situations.

Locate

► Bibles
► Chalk or markers, various colors
► Chalkboard, mural paper, or newsprint
► Paper
► Pencils
► Pointer

Lead

The Psalms are filled with examples of voices crying out to God. Lament psalms are those that call attention to the human condition through the expression of weeping or wailing. Phrases like "Why? How long? Help me," and "Hear my cry" are repeated frequently. Emotions such as sorrow, sadness, loneliness, and fear are spoken and directed to God for a response. The Psalms recognize that only God can restore, reinstate, heal, and comfort. Sometimes the lament psalms ask God to motivate the hearts of humans to accept, to change, to repent, or to be quieted. This activity will help the participants identify ways in which people feel empty, lost, and lowly—especially when precious things like dignity, health, and safety are stripped from them. Through exploring the psalms and writing their own poetry or laments, the participants will express their feelings of being poor in spirit and empathize with those feelings in others.

Introduce the theme of lamenting or grieving by reading Psalm 25. Since there are many additional cries to God throughout the psalms, especially in the first seven chapters, point out more samples for the listeners. Provide Bibles and tell the participants that they will search the book of Psalms to find other examples that express a person's lament. Then, assign each person or team a specific psalm or set of five psalms to scan for phrases and words used to cry out to God or to lament a person's experiences.

Ask the group members to skim their psalm(s) to find words or phrases that indicate lament. As they locate words, tell the learners to go to the chalkboard, mural paper, or newsprint and write them down. Direct the students to fill the space with words, recording them with different colors, angles, and styles rather than forming a column or a list. Model this for the group by printing one phrase at an angle. Remind them that several people can be writing words at the same time.

When the learners have finished searching and writing, read the phrases and words together. Use a pointer to designate the word to read since this will not be apparent from the format. When all of the words have been spoken, ask the group to think about people today who feel this way and what might have been taken from them to make them feel this. Point to a word and lead a discussion on the theme associated with it. Make a list of the situations suggested by the group on another area of the board or on a separate sheet of paper. Examples of suffering could include: someone living with a severe illness; a person who has been physically, emotionally, or verbally abused; one who was robbed or attacked; an individual who has sinned; someone who committed a crime; people experiencing job loss or unemployment; or one who has been betrayed by a loved one.

Next, invite the participants to write their own poems or lament psalms based on one of the situations on the list. Instruct them to write from the perspective of the person who is experiencing the situation. Encourage everyone to think about how the individual would feel, what they might say to God, what they could ask for, and how they might cry out. Remind the group to direct their psalms to God. If desired, the students can use some or all of these phrases to begin lines of their poems:

► O God …

► Help me …

► Hear my cry …

► How …

► Listen to me …

► O Lord, you …

► Why …

When the poems or laments are complete, allow each to be read either by the person who wrote it or by another individual in the class. Take time for a discussion of the theme and for the group to offer specific prayer intentions for those experiencing difficulty in their lives.

Becoming Personally Involved

Acts 6:5
What they said pleased the whole community, and they chose Stephen, a man full of faith and the Holy Spirit.

Learn

Participants will create first-person dramas, or monologues, to share the stories of people who devote their lives to help the poor.

Locate

- Bible
- Biographies of persons who minister to the poor
- Copy machine or printer
- Costume pieces (optional)
- Paper for copy machine or printer
- Pens or pencils
- Props (optional)
- Resource sheet: "First Person Story: Clarence Jordan"

Advance Preparation

- Duplicate a copy of the first person story about Clarence Jordan from the resource sheet and prepare to tell it to the group as a monologue.

Lead

From the earliest history of the church, there have been examples of people who have devoted their lives and spent their resources to help the poor. In Acts 6:5 Stephen is chosen as the first deacon of the church at Jerusalem. In New Testament times, deacons were entrusted with the responsibility of ministering to widows and orphans. Today, deacons—the people commissioned by a particular congregation to serve the needy—are involved with meeting the needs of the poor in many ways. They may collect clothing, distribute food, or provide transportation to those who lack the basics of life. Besides deacons, there are numerous stories of individuals who have given their lives in service to others including Jane Addams, Hull House; Dorothy Day, the Catholic Worker Movement; Millard Fuller, Habitat for Humanity; Clarence Jordan, Koinonia Partners; Martin Luther King, Jr., civil rights advocate; Saint Teresa of Calcutta—Mother Teresa—Missionaries of Charity; and Dan West, Heifer International. These are just a few of the names of individuals or groups who have lived dramatic and well-known lives because of their service. Involve the participants in hearing and telling first person stories, also called monologues, of people who minister in Jesus' name by their words and their deeds.

Continue the lesson by telling the group two first person stories of people who serve the needy. The first monologue is to be of a contemporary person who is known for his or her service to the poor. Use the example of Clarence Jordan, the founder of Koinonia Partners and the author of *Cotton Patch Gospel*, which is provided on the resource sheet. The second account should be of someone known through personal experience who provides aid to those in need. This might be a person in the parish who makes casseroles and serves dinner at a community mission, someone in the neighborhood who provides laundry supplies for women at a day center, or a young person who makes fleece blankets for the homeless.

After the stories are shared, invite the participants to gather information about people who minister to the poor in Jesus' name. These might be biblical or historical figures as well as missionaries sponsored by the congregation or workers in the community. Challenge the learners to prepare first person stories about ordinary people who do extraordinary things, with God's help, to minister to the needy. Explain that a first person story is a dramatic situation portrayed by one actor. In order for the situation to be good drama, the character must be in conflict with another force, God, another person, or him or her self. Effective monologues are usually written in the present tense. Monologues may be performed without costumes or props and theatrical enhancements like lights and sets. Of course, these elements add another dimension to the storytelling, but they are not required.

Direct the pupil's attention to resource materials, such as books, magazines, newspapers, and electronics with internet access, which contain biographies of people who minister to the poor. Invite each student or small group to select a person to use as the basis of a report or, in the interest of time and to assure variety, assign an individual named in the introduction to the lesson to each person or team. If someone wants to compose a drama about a person they know, ask them to share the story with a leader to be sure it is appropriate. Distribute paper and pens or pencils and allow time for the participants to gather interesting facts and to write brief monologues. Contribute additional information and give help where needed. If costumes and props are accessible, make them available to the actors.

Invite each participant or team to present a first person story to the group. Allow time for comments and questions after each monologue. At the conclusion of the lesson, offer a prayer of thanks for people who demonstrate care and concern for the poor.

First Person Story: Clarence Jordan

My name is Clarence Jordan. When I was an ordained Baptist minister, with a PhD in Greek New Testament, I started a ministry in Americus, Georgia that has been in existence since 1942. Koinonia Partners is based on three principles:

1. All people are created equal;

2. People should not fight with each other;

3. All goods should be held in common.

Koinonia exists as a partnership of people working together to minister to each other and to the needs of the poor. Income is produced by growing and selling pecans and fruit cakes, as well as other agricultural products.

In order to make the Gospels more readily available to those in the South, I translated portions of the New Testament into the language of the people. These works include *Cotton Patch Evidence* and *Cotton Patch Versions*. Even though my own church did not understand or appreciate my work, I remained true to my convictions to minister to the poor in Jesus' name, regardless of their color or creed.

Searching for Support

James 2:17
So faith by itself,
if it has no works, is dead.

Learn

Participants will engage in a community scavenger hunt to locate support services for those in need.

Locate

- Bible
- Brochures from agencies that provide services for the poor
- Computer, cell phones, or tablets with internet access
- Copy machine or printer
- Paper for copy machine or printer
- Pens
- Newspapers
- Resource sheet: "Community Services Scavenger Hunt"
- Telephone directories

Advance Preparation

- Arrange transportation for scavenger hunt.
- Enlist adult chaperons and drivers for an offsite activity.
- Duplicate a copy of the scavenger hunt resource sheet for each team.

Lead

Poverty abounds in cities, suburbs, and rural towns. It is even widespread in congregations and schools. For a variety of reasons, such as an increase in single parent families, extended unemployment, and unexpected illness, poverty in the United States continues to rise dramatically. Estimates indicate that one out of every five children in America can be categorized as poor. Creative responses by people of faith are essential in meeting the basic needs of people who require the essentials for life. The words of James 2:14-17 challenge every Christian to get involved! Engage the participants in a scavenger hunt to help them discover community support groups and services available to people who need special services.

Ask the participants to name the types of services and support systems that people with substandard income require. Answers could include: advocacy, clothing, counseling, food, friendship, housing, and medical treatment. Also ask where people might go to meet these needs. Resources could be: after school care programs, clothing distribution points, food pantries, health departments, and youth centers.

Tell the pupils that they will be going on a scavenger hunt. Explain that in a scavenger hunt, individuals or teams are given a list of items to find and a designated time and area in which to locate them. This fun technique is a good method to use to help people learn more about community support groups and services available to the poor. Indicate the procedure for the Scavenger Hunt. It could be played by using the internet and making phone calls to find information; by looking through newspapers, magazines, and brochures and locating names of agencies; or by actually going to suggested sites. If the community is large, assign teams to different areas of the city so the reported information will be as broadly based as possible.

Assign the participants to teams. If the teams are leaving the site and going into the community, arrange for one adult per five students to accompany them.

Distribute a scavenger hunt list to each team. Review the items on the list. In addition to these suggestions, questions could include topics such as: education, holistic support, medical services, spiritual help, transportation, and much more.

Before the groups begin the Scavenger Hunt, review guidelines, set a time limit, share information about locations, and provide resources like agency brochures or computers or phones with internet access. Answer any questions that will clarify the procedure.

When the teams have finished the Scavenger Hunt, have one representative from each group share their results. Compile the information into a resource file for future reference or for use in the church or school office.

Use the words of James 2:14-17 to challenge the participants to become involved in starting or supporting programs that minister to men, women, and children in need.

Community Services Scavenger Hunt

▶ Bring brochures from three agencies that offer counseling services to families living in poverty.

▶ Come up with five congregations that offer support to the poor. List the names of the contact persons and the type of help available.

▶ Create a list of three youth service projects that are educating and supporting at-risk teens. Describe the programs offered.

▶ Discover five community resource groups that offer substance abuse and treatment services.

▶ Find four organizations that supply basic needs such as food, clothing, and shelter to the poor. Interview a worker at each location and write a short paragraph about the services provided.

▶ Get information about support groups for the unemployed. List meeting times and services offered.

▶ Go to a library and record the titles of ten books on poverty related subjects.

▶ Locate information about two organizations that offer support and services for children living at the poverty level. Describe the programs provided.

▶ Make a list of three organizations that offer advocacy programs. Services could include legal representation and paperwork processing. Supply name of group, contact person, address, phone number, and list of services

▶ Record phone numbers and hours for three sites that offer after school care. Supply information on costs and programs.

Encouraging through Music

1 Thessalonians 5:11

Therefore encourage one another
and build up each other,
as indeed you are doing.

Learn

Participants will listen to the lyrics of music
that builds positive self-image.

Locate

► Bible

► Equipment to play music

► Recordings of music that promotes
  positive self esteem

Advance Preparation

► Prior to the session, invite the participants
  to each bring or select at least one
  example of a classic or a contemporary
  song with words which build self-esteem.

► Search for "contemporary music that
  promotes self image" and compile a
  playlist for the session.

Lead

Poor, in the sense that Jesus describes
in Matthew 25, can take many forms. A
person who has lost dignity or self-worth
can be considered poor, especially poor in
spirit. Positive feelings of acceptance and
appreciation are treasures which should be
promoted and protected. Unfortunately,
young people often struggle to feel valued.
Negative comments, put downs, and
criticism are given and received every day.
Positive and negative messages have many
sources, one of them being the lyrics of
songs. In this activity, participants will share
a variety of music which affects their spirit
and can help overcome feelings of
being poor in spirit.

Ask the group to recall music that they heard
or sang as a young child which made them
feel good about themselves. These may be
songs from television shows they watched at
home, pre-school programs they attended,
or early church experiences like Sunday
School, camp, or Vacation Bible School.
Students might remember Mister Rogers'
opening music "It's a Beautiful Day In This
Neighborhood," Barney's "I Love You" theme
song, or the classic children's hymn "Jesus
Loves Me." Take time to recall some of these
songs and enjoy singing parts of them
as a group.

Read 1 Thessalonians 5:11. Talk about how it
makes the learners feel when someone says
unkind or uncomplimentary things to them.
Contrast those emotions with how it feels to
be encouraged or affirmed by
another person.

Ask the participants to name songs which communicate that they are unique, valuable, and special. Include songs which tell the group members that God created and cares about them. Spend time sharing the recordings which were brought by the students and the leader.

Remind the group that there are countless examples of music that does not promote self-worth. Too many songs strip people of their value and make them feel incapable, incompetent, and put down. Songs which do not respect life, which present a one-dimensional view of boys and girls or men and women, or which devalue a particular class, culture, ethnic, or religious group are examples. Talk about the ways in which these types of songs could rob the listener and make him or her feel poor in spirit.

Conclude the class by playing a song with a positive message of self-worth. Challenge the students to choose music to share with their friends and to listen to themselves which will minister positively to their spirits, build their self-image, overcome the negative messages they receive daily, and enable them to use their gifts in service of others.

Addressing Unemployment

Psalm 90:17

Let the favor of the Lord our God be upon us, and prosper for us the work of our hands—O prosper the work of our hands!

Learn

Participants will conduct a survey to learn about unemployment issues and create a weaving to illustrate how the factors are interconnected.

Locate

- ► Bible
- ► Chalk or markers
- ► Chalkboard or newsprint
- ► Glue
- ► Paper
- ► Paper, 12" x 18" construction
- ► Paper cutter (optional)
- ► Pencils or pens
- ► Ruler
- ► Scissors
- ► Tacks or tape, masking

Advance Preparation

- ► Cut construction paper into 1" x 12" strips. At least eight to ten pieces are needed for each participant.

Lead

Addressing issues concerning unemployment is an important aspect of learning to minister to the poor. Many of the experiences related to being without a job are common among all people who face this difficult situation. Help the participants learn more about the factors facing the unemployed by conducting surveys, making weavings to illustrate how the concerns are interconnected, and praying for those in need of work.

Introduce the theme of the session, unemployment, and read the passage from Psalm 90:17. Invite the group to offer definitions of the word unemployment. Unemployed means to be without a job. Ask the students to name some of the causes, or reasons, for unemployment. Suggestions could include economic factors, educational background, and seasonal cycles, as well as addiction issues, health concerns, and technological advances.

Tell the participants that they will be conducting surveys to determine factors related to unemployment that are common among people without a job. Explain that a survey is an information gathering tool that records opinions, but not necessarily facts. Distribute paper and pencils or pens. Discuss basic issues related to unemployment.

Have the participants print one or two questions at the top of their paper such as:

- ► What are some of the causes of unemployment?
- ► What are some problems faced by the unemployed?
- ► What are some of the things that people lose when they are unemployed?

Note that the surveyors may wish to help people expand their answers by asking "Why?" or "What can be done to address that need?"

Provide the guidelines for the activity. Tell the group who they will be contacting, such as members of the congregation, families and friends, or persons in the neighborhood or community. State if the participants will work alone, in pairs, or as small groups, and form teams, if necessary. If transportation is involved, note where the group will be going and how they will get there. Set the time limit for the project. Clarify the directions and answer questions. Allow time for this portion of the activity. As an alternative, if the entire project is to be completed within one session, arrange for people from the congregation or school such as another class or the parents to be present and serve as a test group for the survey.

Once the surveys are completed, ask the participants to share the results. Record common themes on a chalkboard or a piece of newsprint. Problems might include benefits, finances, housing, insurance, medical care, pensions, savings, and vacations. Responses related to losses could be dignity, emotions, friends, networking, plans, purpose, self-worth, and sense of accomplishment. Discuss any of the information that needs to be expanded or explained.

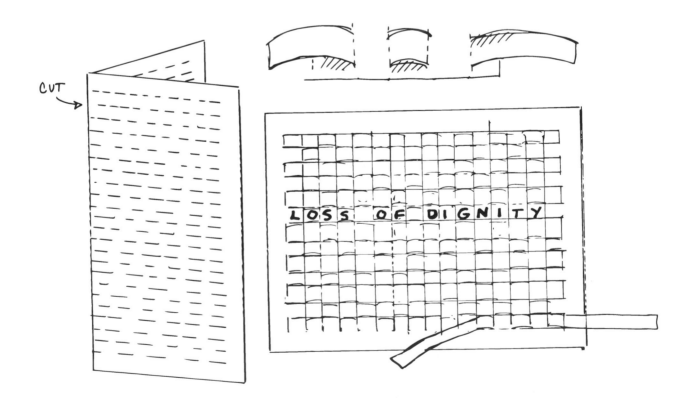

Tell the learners that they will select themes, write them on strips of paper, and create weavings. Through the weaving activity, the participants will discover that the various components of unemployment are interconnected. Encourage variety in the topics, and help the group members select issues and concerns to use in their project.

Demonstrate the procedure for making the woven mat. Fold a 12" x 18" piece of construction paper in half horizontally. Pencil a margin line one inch from the open edges of the paper, opposite the fold. Cut slits into the folded edge, spacing them one inch apart. Be certain to stop cutting at the margin line. Then open the paper and lay it flat. Cut colored strips, one inch by twelve inches. Using pen or marker, write one unemployment related factor on each strip. Begin weaving the pieces under and over the slits in the paper. Each row alternates, if row one begins under, then row two starts over and so on until the colored strips are woven across the entire width, forming a mat. Fasten any loose ends with a little glue. Provide the supplies and guide the students as they weave the mats.

When the weavings are completed, tape or tack the mats to a bulletin board or wall. Ask each student to stand near his or her project. Tell the group to reflect on the various aspects of unemployment, and to imagine themselves in the situation. Ask which factor would affect them the most. Take turns offering sentence prayers for persons in those particular situations. For example, "I pray for someone whose dreams have been shattered," or "I remember the family that does not have money for rent." Conclude by inviting the pupils to take their weavings home, use them as placemats or table decorations, and continue remembering unemployed people in their daily prayers.

Giving for the Poor

Mark 12:42

A poor widow came and put in two small copper coins, which are worth a penny.

Learn

Participants will recall the Bible story of the widow's mite and construct bottle puppets to share accounts of organizations that use pennies to help the poor.

Locate

► Bag, small paper
► Bible
► Bottles, colored plastic – 1 per person or group
► Cotton, fake fur, or yarn
► Fabric
► Felt scraps
► Glue, fabric or tacky
► Paper tubes, 1 per person
► Pennies, enough to fill one small paper bag
► Scissors
► Tape, duct

Advance Preparation

► Fill a small paper bag with pennies.
► Wash the plastic bottles and remove the labels.

Lead

Many times people pass by a penny on the sidewalk or in the street because it is not worth the trouble to stop and pick it up. In the New Testament story of the widow's mite, Mark 12:41-44, a woman gave her smallest coin—the one worth the least amount of money - yet her generosity was praised. Of course, one penny does not buy much or go far. Yet, a penny, combined with other pennies, can do great things. In this lesson, the students will learn about organizations that use pennies to help the poor. They will make a "puppet for pennies" from recycled materials and develop skits about people who have been helped by these groups.

Invite the students to sit in a circle on the floor. Hold up a bag filled with pennies and tell the students that it is a bag of seeds. Run one hand through the pennies or shake the sack and ask them to guess what kind of seeds they think are in the container. When someone says that they are pennies, show the group a handful of coins. Ask what pennies can be used to grow. When there are several suggestions, tell the group that pennies, like seeds, can be used to grow many wonderful things.

Explain that charitable organizations collect pennies and use the donated coins to support projects that help poor people in many different ways. Some groups build hospitals and schools, others provide clothing and food, and still others protect the health of children around the world. Anyone can help with projects like these. Just like the widow who only had a mite—two small coins - it only takes a penny given in love to make a big difference! Present information about some of the groups which use change in helpful ways.

- **UNICEF**—United Nations International Children's Emergency Fund. UNICEF provides free immunizations and vaccines for children around the world as well as many other kinds of medical help for boys and girls who would otherwise not receive it. The donations collected from programs like Halloween Trick or Treating supports these efforts in many countries.

- **Project Heifer** - Heifer collects pennies to provide live animals for people around the world. The recipients breed the animals and soon have a flock of chickens or sheep, a herd of cows or goats, or a school of fish. The receivers then give a pair of animals to another family or person to breed. In this way everyone who receives the animals has an on-going supply of food.

- **Least Coin**—Many service and social groups from around the world participate in a program called Least Coin. At each meeting they collect their nation's "least coin" - the one with the lowest monetary value - from members. At year-end all donations are combined with the "pennies" from other groups. Funds are spent to build hospitals and schools in countries where they are desperately needed.

Some churches and schools plan their own projects. During "Thankful for Teeth," people pay a dime for every tooth they have to thank God for this blessing. A dentist from the community uses the collected money to help children have dental care. "Nickels for Nails" buys supplies for a Habitat for Humanity home. The "Change for Change Challenge" encourages folks to fill a large container with coins and the money is used to repair homes during a mission to Appalachia.

After reviewing the projects, organize the participants into groups of four persons to construct bottle puppets and create stories. Tell them that each team is to develop a skit based on the experiences of people who have been helped by the pennies collected by others. Assign or suggest one of the following themes or have the groups develop one of their own.

Examples include:

- a family living in a house built or fixed by people from a church;
- a household who received a calf from Project Heifer;
- children who were given life saving and protecting immunizations by UNICEF;
- young people attending a school built by Least Coin.

Instruct the group members to plan their skits. Each should choose a country where the story takes place, the characters for the scenario, as well as the actions they will portray. When each team has a plan, the learners can create puppets to play the various parts.

Demonstrate the process for making a bottle rod puppet. Turn a plastic bottle upside down and use duct tape to attach a paper towel tube to the pouring spout. This will serve as the rod by which the puppet is operated. Next use felt scraps to make facial features. Two to three layered colors will form effective eyes. The handle of the bottle becomes the nose. Add a mouth under the handle.

Make hair for the puppet using cotton, fake fur, or yarn. Alternately, cloth could be cut into strips and glued in place. The creators may prefer to make a hat or headpiece which is worn in the country in which their play takes place. Form a basic costume using a rectangle of fabric. Fold the material in quarters and cut a small hole at the point. Slide the hole up the rod of the puppet and turn the character upside down. Use duct tape to secure the fabric in place. Tape the fabric on the inside, covering the tape which was previously used to attach the rod. Turn the puppet right side up and use other fabrics to add additional decorations to the clothing.

Provide the puppet-making materials and allow time for the teams to construct their characters and practice their skits. When all groups are ready, present the plays for each other. If possible, invite parents, members of the congregation, or children in other classes to view the presentations. Ask for a donation of a coin from each person in the audience. Choose one of the agencies studied and donate the collection to that group.

Celebrating the Caring

Luke 6:30

Give to everyone who begs from you; and if anyone takes away your goods, do not ask for them again.

Learn

Participants will hear the story of St. Martin of Tours and celebrate Martinmas in honor of his commitment to the poor.

Locate

- ▶ Bible
- ▶ Candle holders
- ▶ Candles
- ▶ Cupcakes or cake mix and ingredients
- ▶ Cups
- ▶ Equipment for making cupcakes and frosting
- ▶ Food coloring, orange and yellow, or fruit slices
- ▶ Forks
- ▶ Frosting
- ▶ Juice
- ▶ Knives
- ▶ Matches
- ▶ Napkins
- ▶ Plates

Advance Preparation

- ▶ Bake cupcakes ahead of time or purchase unfrosted cupcakes.
- ▶ Prepare frosting, leaving some white and tinting some with orange and yellow food coloring.

Lead

Since the beginning of time God has called special people to help with God's work in the world. Saint Martin of Tours, a fourth century bishop in France, learned this lesson as a young boy. A legend repeated each year on November 11, Saint Martin's feast day, recalls the need to care for others. In this activity learners will hear about St. Martin and participate in a Martinmas observance. They will create a party to celebrate the actions of St. Martin and others who give their lives to help the poor.

Share the legend of St. Martin of Tours. As a young man, Martin passed through an archway in the city where he lived. Under the passage he saw a poor beggar shivering in the cold. The homeless man was almost naked, having few clothes to keep him warm. Martin took off his cape, tore it in half, and gave a portion of it to the poor man to keep him warm. The next night Martin had a dream in which Christ appeared. In it Jesus was wearing the piece of cape which Martin had given to the beggar. Then Martin understood that even when helping the poorest of people he was really helping Christ. Martin became a bishop and is today the patron saint of beggars and outcasts, those who are sometimes called homeless and vagrants.

In France, November 11 is known as Martinmas, or St. Martin's feast day. His life is celebrated with a simple cake. Also, a festival of lanterns is held, with light carried throughout the rooms of a darkened house to recall how Saint Martin brought light to many people who experienced only darkness in their lives.

Invite the group to share in preparing a Martinmas celebration. Have the participants frost the cupcakes with white icing. Then have them use the orange and yellow frosting to design a sun on the top of each cupcake. Fruit slices could also be used to create the symbol on the treats. Set the table for the party with napkins and plates. Pour cups of juice and set one at each place.

When the group is ready for the celebration, ask the participants to name other people who have dedicated their lives to helping the poor. State that these could be biblical, historical, and contemporary examples. Light a candle as a symbol for each person mentioned and set it in the center of the table. Just before serving the cupcakes, read Luke 6:30-31, as an opening prayer. Encourage the listeners to hear and follow those important words. Enjoy the Martinmas celebration the group has created together.

Responding to Needs

Romans 15:26

For Macedonia and Achaia have been pleased to share their resources with the poor among the saints at Jerusalem.

Learn

Participants will consider unexpected situations that create needs and depict solutions on a patchwork quilt.

Locate

- ► Bible
- ► Fabric
- ► Iron (optional)
- ► Ironing board (optional)
- ► Markers - permanent, paint markers, or liquid embroidery pens
- ► Material for backing (optional)
- ► Pole or rod (optional)
- ► Scissors
- ► Sewing equipment
- ► Wonder Under fusible web (optional)

Advance Preparation

- ► Cut a 4" x 4" or larger fabric square per person.
- ► Arrange for a parent or member of the congregation or community to sew the completed fabric squares together to form a quilt.

Lead

Unfortunately, poverty often comes in unexpected and unexplained ways. People are stripped of material possessions and money in a matter of hours as a hurricane strikes, in a duration of months as medical bills mount, and over a period of years as retirement income declines. Paul's words in the letter to the Romans tells how the Christians in the early church shared their material possessions with the citizens of Jerusalem who faced difficult times following a famine. Their example challenges followers of Christ in any age to share God's love by meeting the needs of people in difficult situations and circumstances. Through making a patchwork quilt that illustrates ways in which God's love is shared with people in need, the participants will become more aware of how they too can participate in this important ministry of service.

Introduce the activity and the theme for the project. Tell the participants that they will be working together to make a patchwork quilt that illustrates ways of sharing God's love with people in need because of unexpected situations. Read Romans 15:25-26. Explain that there had been a famine in Jerusalem. Paul was commending the Christian communities in Achaia and Macedonia for reaching out and meeting the needs of the hungry in Jerusalem.

As a group, brainstorm ways in which children, youth, and adults today become people in need in unexpected ways. Examples might be through accidents, floods, hurricanes, illness, tornadoes, unemployment, war, and many other ideas. Rather than concentrating on how a person or group has become poor, emphasize ways in which Christians can respond to meet the needs of people in these difficult situations. For example, if a person's home has been damaged because of a tornado, an organization might repair the residence. If a person has lost income because of an illness, a congregation may collect money to provide medical care. Remind the students to list concrete solutions to specific disasters. The ideas will make up the content of each person's patchwork quilt square.

After each student has listed his or her own suggestion, distribute the fabric patches and the permanent markers, liquid embroidery pens, or paint markers. Tell the participants to decorate their squares with meaningful designs, scenes, symbols, or words to represent their responses.

When the students have finished decorating the squares, determine how they will be arranged by laying them out on the floor or on a table. Sew the patches together by hand or by machine, or iron onto a background using a bonding material such as Wonder Under. If a finished back is desired, cut a plain piece of fabric the size of the finished banner to use for a backing. Place right sides together. Stitch the backing to the patchwork, leaving the bottom end open. Turn right side out. Slip stitch the bottom end.

If the patchwork piece is to be used as a banner, stitch a casing or add loops to the top of the cloth. Insert a pole or rod for hanging the work.

Display the completed patchwork piece in a prominent place to remind the participants, and the congregation or school, of their commitment to share God's love with people in need.

If desired, arrange an auction to sell the banner or quilt. Donate the profits to an organization that provides relief to those suffering the effects of sudden or long-term disasters.

Helping the Homeless

Isaiah 58:7

Is it not to share your bread with the hungry, and bring the homeless poor into your house; when you see the naked, to cover them, and not to hide yourself from your own kin?

Learn

Participants will learn about homelessness and respond by creating paper bag cartoons suggesting actions to make a difference

Locate

► Bag, large paper with handles

► Bags, large brown paper grocery type

► Bible

► Book - *Benjamin Brody's Backyard Bag* (Wezeman, Phyllis Vos and Colleen Aalsburg Wiessner. Elgin, IL: Brethren Press, 1991.)

► Markers

► Resources on homelessness

► Tape, masking

Advance Preparation

► Obtain a copy of the children's book on homelessness, *Benjamin Brody's Backyard Bag*, from a bookstore, library, or from the distributor:

The Pastoral Center
844-727-8672
resources@pastoralcenter.com
www.pastoral.center

Lead

Homelessness is a justice issue that affects millions of people. It is a complex problem with many causes. People may become homelessness for reasons such as alcohol or drug abuse, divorce, high housing costs, limited income, serious mental illness, a natural disaster, and unemployment. In this lesson, participants will explore the multi-faceted issue of homelessness by creating cartoons and suggesting plans to help address this difficult situation.

Introduce the subject of homelessness by displaying a large, paper shopping bag with handles. Invite the participants to brainstorm some of the ways in which a bag can be used. With a marker, record these ideas on one side of the sack. Suggestions may include carrying groceries home from the store, filling it with books, and turning it into a costume. If no one mentions that homeless people sometimes use a bag to carry their possessions, talk about the fact that for some children, youth, and adults, a bag is a home. Add the word home to the list on the shopping bag.

Show the class the book *Benjamin Brody's Backyard Bag* and tell them that it is a children's story about homelessness. Read the book to the group or summarize it in the following way:

Once a little boy named Benjamin Brody discovers many creative uses for a bag. It becomes a garage for his toy cars, a tablecloth for a lunchtime picnic, and a net for catching butterflies. On a walk with his mother and sister, Benjamin notices a woman sitting on a park bench sorting through items in a large paper shopping bag. Benjamin thought that she must be playing his game, too. After talking with the woman, however, Benjamin discovers that she was not playing a game. In fact, for her, the bag was her home.

After finishing the story, turn the shopping bag over. Invite the participants to think of ways in which a bag can be used to help homeless people. Print the suggestions on the blank side of the bag. For example, they could fill a bag with blankets, clothes, food, and toiletries that can be donated to an agency that aids the homeless.

Next, tell the group that they will be drawing cartoons to illustrate ways to help the homeless. A cartoon is a drawing that often exaggerates or simplifies the theme to make a point. Illustrations in a cartoon may be as basic as line drawings and stick figures. Distribute a brown paper grocery bag to each person. Place markers within sharing distance of the students. Instruct each person to use a marker to divide the paper into four equal sections and to write one of the following words in each quarter of the bag: World, Nation, State, Community.

Instruct the group to draw a cartoon in each square that illustrates one solution to homelessness for that particular theme. For example:

- **World**: Collect blankets for Church World Service to distribute to people around the world to provide shelter as well as warmth.

- **Nation**: Help a family build their own home with an organization like Habitat for Humanity.

- **State**: Write letters to advocate for state taxes to provide medical services to the poor

- **Community**: Gather items and prepare "Comfort Kits" of basic necessities like a comb, shampoo, soap, toothbrush, and toothpaste to give to homeless centers.

Indicate the resource materials on homelessness that are available online and in printed form for the students to use during the activity. Allow time for this portion of the project.

When the cartoons are completed, tape each bag to a wall. When all participants have posted a sheet, invite the group to walk through the "art gallery" to learn more about ways to help the homeless. Encourage everyone to browse, read, and note interesting ideas. After a brief time, invite each person to stand by his or her bag. Take turns having people introduce themselves by name and tell one thing that they would like others to remember about addressing homelessness. Affirm the suggestions that have been shared by the class. Challenge each person to turn his or her idea into action by becoming involved in a project or program related to homelessness.

I WAS SICK

Christians model their care of the sick after the example of Jesus. Throughout his ministry Jesus reached out in compassion to those who struggled with physical, emotional, and spiritual illness. He entered the world of those whose disease cut them off from society, he healed many who came to him in faith, and he comforted individuals whose lives had been shattered by circumstances or events. In the gospels Jesus offers little explanation for why people suffer from sickness. Rather, Jesus met illness with action. He listened to the person's story, he forgave them of their sins, and he healed them of their ailments.

Christians learn from Jesus' response to illness and are challenged to act accordingly. Our concern can take many forms: encouragement for organizations that work with the dying; support for research to discover cures for diseases which still elude us; educational campaigns to combat illnesses that can be prevented; direct care of the sick in many situations. Following Christ's example, we can be alert and available to those around us who experience a lack of health and wholeness in a wide variety of ways.

A traditional action or work of mercy is to visit the sick. One who visits the ill is a sign of the larger community's care. A person who visits the sick brings with him or her the expression of hope rooted in the good news of Christ.

As with other merciful works, responding to the needs of the sick takes forms other than caring for physical illness. Emotional and spiritual illness permeate all ages, classes, and cultures of people today. Jesus said that those who bring comfort to individuals whose lives have been emotionally or spiritually devastated by circumstances or events will likewise be rewarded.

The activities of this chapter will help the students to act on Jesus' direction to provide care for the sick, Matthew 25:36-44. "When did we see you ill?" those on Jesus' right hand asked him. And he responded, "Whatever you did for one of the least of these who are members of my family, you did it for me." By responding to Jesus' challenge, we gain assurance that we will someday hear Christ's words, "I was sick and you took care of me."

Chart

Title	Scripture	Theme	Activity/Method	Page
Overview	▶ Matthew 25:36b, 39a, 43c, 44b	▶ Sick		147
Sending a Caring Message	▶ Psalm 25:16	▶ Care Facility or Homebound	▶ Art: Fabric Stitched Card	150
Identifying the Feelings	▶ Matthew 5:4	▶ Heartsickness	▶ Creative Writing: Journal ▶ Drama: Mime	152
Focusing on Feelings	▶ Philippians 4:4-8	▶ Emotions/ Illness	▶ Creative Writing: Healing Prayers ▶ Drama: Freeze Frames ▶ Game: Matching Emotions/ Illness	154
Meeting Special Needs	▶ Hebrews 12:1	▶ Physical Challenges	▶ Game: Go Fish	158
Creating Recipes for Healthy Living	▶ 1 Corinthians 6:19	▶ Eating/Food Addictions/ Issues	▶ Creative Writing: Recipes for Healthy Living	161
Uplifting the Sick	▶ Psalm 23 ▶ Psalm 46 ▶ Psalm 103:1-5 ▶ Psalm 118:4-5 ▶ Psalm 139:7-14 ▶ Isaiah 40:30-31 ▶ Isaiah 43:1-3a ▶ Jeremiah 29:11-13 ▶ Luke 4:18-21 ▶ James 5:13-14	▶ Accident	▶ Art: Poster ▶ Creative Writing: Prayer Marathon	165
Proclaiming the Message	▶ Psalm 100:5	▶ Choices That Impact Children	▶ Creative Writing: Public Service Announcement ▶ Puppetry: Paper Tube Rod Puppet	172

Ministering In Mercy	► Matthew 5:7	► Organizations/ Terminally Ill Children	► Art: Pennant ► Creative Writing: Letters	175
Taking Care of the Sick	► Matthew 25:36b	► Caregiving	► Banners/Textiles: Pocket Banner	179
Portraying Health Issues	► Luke 10:25-37	► Health Care	► Art: Cooperative Cartoon ► Creative Writing: Word Web	181

Sending a Caring Message

Psalm 25:16
Turn to me and be gracious to me,
for I am lonely and afflicted.

Learn

Participants will remember people who are in a care facility or homebound by making and sending fabric stitched cards.

Locate

- ► Basket or manila envelope
- ► Bible
- ► Envelopes
- ► Fabric such as calico, gingham, or other small print or plain colored material
- ► Iron
- ► Ironing board
- ► Markers, fine point permanent
- ► Paper, cardstock
- ► Pencils
- ► Pens
- ► Postage stamps (optional)
- ► Scissors
- ► Wonder Under fusible web

Advance Preparation

- ► Arrange for an adult to assist with ironing, if desired.
- ► Cut the cardstock paper into a size to match the envelopes that will be used.
- ► Iron the Wonder Under fusible web onto the back of a variety of pieces of material. It is available in craft and fabric stores and a full set of instructions is attached to each piece.
- ► Obtain names and addresses from the church office or a healthcare facility, hospice, or retirement community of people who are homebound or in an extended care center. If privacy regulations do not allow giving out personal information, explain the project and ask if the cards may be dropped off for distribution to patients and residents.

Lead

Serious illness suffered in isolation from a caring community is a double trauma. Not only are the effects of the illness physically wearing, but lack of contact with others can add to feelings of anxiety, despair, and loneliness. In every city and town—rural and urban—many people are isolated in their homes or in care centers because of a physical condition or a disability. While most of these people are elderly, an increasing number of young people require long-term care because of accidents or serious illnesses. Those in your group may personally know someone in this situation today. This activity will offer participants an opportunity to reach out to these people by making and sending cards with messages of care and hope, which will help the recipients feel connected with others.

Ask the participants to imagine what it would be like to be homebound or institutionalized—without family and friends nearby—because of a physical disability or an illness. Consider the needs of these people and how they could be met. After time for discussion, ask the group to brainstorm solutions to the problems introduced by the questions and responses. Summarize by pointing out that people who are homebound with an illness often become lonely and discouraged and feel cut off from other people. Explain that they might feel like David did when he wrote Psalm 25:16. Read the verse to the group. Discuss how the psalmist represents these same feelings.

Tell the participants that they are going to make greeting cards to send to people who are homebound (someone they know or others they don't know) or who are living in a convalescent home or hospice. Emphasize the importance of writing messages that are cheerful, but not silly; caring, but not depressing. If available, give each participant the name and address of the person they will write. Have them pen a few sample messages on scratch paper and then share them with the group. Check for appropriateness. Next, explain that the front of the cards will be decorated to look like the designs have been sewn in place. Distribute pencils, scissors, and a piece of fabric backed with Wonder Under fusible web to each participant. Ask them to cut out decorations from the fabric like balloons, flowers, hearts, or letters to spell simple words such as hello or love.

Next, have the participants arrange the fabric cutouts on the front of the cardstock. When the design is ready, demonstrate how to

iron it in place. Make sure the steam setting on the iron is off. Supervise the students as they use the iron. If necessary, allow each to arrange the design on the card front and then have an adult iron it in place for a young person.

Demonstrate how to use fine point markers to create the appearance of stitching along the edges of the fabric. Space little marks, approximately one-fourth inch in length, evenly apart starting on the fabric and extending out onto the paper. The markers can also be used to draw balloon strings or to finish other necessary parts of the design.

Complete the project by having the artists print or write a message on the inside of their card. Words could be chosen from the list developed by the group. A simple poem or verse from a Psalm would also be appropriate. Instruct the students to sign their names to their card and address the envelope.

When the cards are finished, place them in a basket or a large manila envelope. Gather in a circle around them. Say a simple prayer based on Psalm 25:16, "Dear God, use our messages of caring to be gracious to those who are lonely and afflicted. Help all those who receive these greetings to know that you are with them and that your family of faith remembers and cares about them. We offer this prayer in Jesus' name. Amen."

Deliver or mail the cards individually or in the large envelope.

Identifying the Feelings

Matthew 5:4
'Blessed are those who mourn,
for they will be comforted.'

Learn

Participants will explore the theme of heartsickness and learn to express feelings through journal writing and mime.

Locate

▶ Bible

▶ Box

▶ Cards, 3" x 5"

▶ Chalk or marker

▶ Chalkboard or newsprint

▶ Paper, notebook

▶ Pencils or pens

Lead

Although the word heartsick might not be found in a medical dictionary, it is an ailment that is experienced by people of all ages. Heartsickness generally involves a loss, which can range from something as concrete as misplacing something valuable to something as abstract as losing a way of life. It could be triggered by the loss of a close friend who moves to another city or by the end of a familiar routine at the close of a school term. Since heartsickness involves many emotions, young people can grow from their experiences by learning to express their feelings. In this lesson participants will explore the theme of heartsickness though the use of mime and journal writing.

Explain that feelings are as much a part of a person as fingers and toes, yet they are often much less obvious and need more clarification. When discussing and dealing with situations involving heartsickness, feelings play an important role. A student who has a sibling with a terminal illness may be angry that his or her brother or sister might die at a young age. A young person with parents in the process of a divorce could be scared. Someone with a failing grade might be bitter about not being allowed to participate in extra-curricular activities. Part of the process of dealing with the issues related to heartsickness is learning to identify and express feelings. This requires practice and participation.

Gather the pupils in a circle. Ask each learner, in turn, to name a feeling. As the feeling, such as angry, confused, happy, sad, or surprised is named, write each word on a separate card and place it in the box. Suggest additional feelings if the players run out of ideas. Ask one person at a time to pick a card from the box and to pantomime the feeling written on it through facial expressions and body gestures. There should be no talking. Invite the remaining learners to guess the feeling. Continue until everyone has had a turn.

Tell the group that people who experience various types of losses confront many different emotions. Discuss a variety of situations and circumstances and ask those gathered to name, describe, or mime feelings that are specifically associated with them. Use these suggestions as guidelines for the activity:

► Blake's dog has run away;
► Dionne has lost 20 dollars;
► Krista can't find her house key.

In these three common occurrences of loss, Dionne might be feeling angry that he can't find his money, Blake is concerned because her dog is gone, and Krista may be fearful that she will get in trouble for losing the key.

Try these situations with the group:

► Hope's father has lost his job;
► Marla is moving to a new city;
► Suk Lee has an accident and his car is damaged.

Help the participants distinguish and discuss the many feelings associated with each of these scenarios and others such as divorce, fire, and illness.

Conclude this portion of the activity by reminding the students that everyone experiences feelings, and that it is important to identify and express emotions in order to deal with them concretely and constructively. One way to do this is through the use of "I" statements. Explain that an "I" statement is a personal expression of feelings. For example, "When I lost my math book, I felt scared that I would be in trouble with my teacher."

Start the students on a journal writing project as a way to help them explore themes associated with heartsickness and as practice in using "I" statements to express their feelings. A journal is a daily, or periodic, record of events and the emotions associated with them. Explain the project and inspire the group to use their personal pages as a way to communicate thoughts and feelings

and to explore problems and possible solutions. Tell the group that although writing words is a good way to journal, art work on the pages is also encouraged.

Distribute notebook paper and pens or pencils. Ask each participant to reflect on one or more topics associated with heartsickness. These could be real or imaginary situations. Sentence starters, prepared in advance or suggested by the group, may be written on a chalkboard or a piece of newsprint and the students may select phrases to use in their journals.

Examples are:

► A best friend moves to another city;
► A brother or sister has a serious illness;
► A car accident;
► A grandparent dies;
► A natural disaster such as a flood or a tornado;
► A new school;
► A parent loses a job;
► A pet dies;
► A student is not selected for a team.

After each person has chosen a situation, encourage the students to write in their journals trying to capture their feelings, emotions, and experiences. Remind the group to use "I" statements in their writing. Tell the group that although this is a personal project, they have the option of sharing their thoughts and feelings with each other. If desired, allow time for a one-on-one or large group exchange of the writing projects. Encourage the learners to continue to use journal writing to express their feelings about the situations they encounter every day.

Focusing on Feelings

Philippians 4:6
Do not worry about anything, but in everything by prayer and supplication with thanksgiving let your requests be made known to God.

Learn

Participants will make a connection between emotions and illness, act out feelings, and offer prayers for people experiencing those situations.

Locate

- ▶ Bible
- ▶ Copy machine or printer
- ▶ Paper for copy machine or printer
- ▶ Pencils or pens
- ▶ Resource sheet: "Feeling Words"
- ▶ Resource sheet: "Healing Prayers"

Advance Preparation

- ▶ Duplicate a copy of the Feeling Words resource sheet for each person.
- ▶ Make a copy of the Healing Prayers resource sheet for each participant or small group.

Lead

Medical discoveries indicate a strong connection between emotional anxiety and stress and mental and physical health conditions. Research indicates that negative emotions can make people ill if allowed to dominate their lives. In this activity students will look at some possible links between emotions and symptoms of mental and physical illness. They will portray the feelings through freeze-frame dramas and then pray for the people who struggle with these emotions.

Read Philippians 4:4-8 to the group. Comment on how difficult those words are to follow. Ask the participants to suggest negative emotions which can dominate someone's life. They may name anger, fear, hatred, or worry. Talk about how various states of mind can affect the mental and physical health of people who harbor them. Offer examples such as they have frequent headaches, some become depressed, and others develop a chronic illness.

Distribute the list of emotions and illnesses/symptoms to each student. Take a few minutes to read through the list and define any words that needs explanation. Offer pencils or pens and tell the group members to draw a line from a negative emotion to a physical problem which it may cause. Though the answers may vary, tell the students to try to use all of the entries in both columns. Some emotions may be linked to several physical symptoms and some symptoms to a variety of feelings.

After the connections have been made, ask individuals, pairs, or trios to choose a word from the list. Tell them that they will portray the emotion for the group in a freeze-frame format. Explain that they are to act out the feeling and then freeze in place for a few minutes as a prayer is read for people who face that situation. Give the actors time to plan how they will convey the emotion. When they are prepared, have the group sit in a circle.

Pass out a Healing Prayers handout to each person. Note that the students will take turns stepping into the middle of the circle, displaying their emotion, and freezing in place while the rest of the group says a prayer for people who face the situation. A moment of silence should follow each prayer sentence, giving individuals in the group an opportunity to silently pray for people they know who struggle with the negative emotion which has been named.

Begin and end each segment with the words "Dear Lord, heal our minds and emotions so that our bodies may also be whole."

Name the first emotion, such as stress, and ask the individual or group that prepared it to come to the center of the circle. Recite the opening sentence together. Have the performers act out the feeling word and freeze in place. Direct the rest of the participants to read the prayer for stress together. Pause for a few seconds of silent reflection. Conclude with the unison sentence. Repeat the process for each emotion on the list.

Conclude the lesson by repeating the prayer: "Dear Lord, heal our minds and emotions so that our bodies may also be whole." Spend a few moments in silence before the group is dismissed.

Feeling Words

Anger	Asthma
Fear	Cancer
Concern about the Past	Depression
Grudge	Exhaustion
Holding in Feelings	Headache
Jealousy	Heart Attack
Obsession with a Mistake	High Blood Pressure
Resentment	Loss of Appetite
Sadness	Stroke
Stress	Suppressed Immune System
Worry	Ulcer

Healing Prayers

Opening and Closing Prayer

Dear Lord, heal our minds and emotions so that our bodies may also be whole.

Anger

God, help those who are filled with anger to be able to let go of it for their own sake and for yours.

Concern about the Past

Dear God, thank you that you are always willing to give us a fresh start. Free those who are unable to let go of the past.

Fear

Prince of Peace, give your peace to those whose lives are ruled by fear.

Grudge

Dear Lord, be close to those who are holding grudges. Help them to be able to give and to receive forgiveness.

Holding in Feelings

O Lord, give freedom to those who are locked in a prison of their own feelings. Help them to learn to express what they feel in helpful ways.

Jealousy

Giver of all good gifts, give the gifts of gratitude and acceptance to those who feel only envy and jealousy.

Obsession with a Mistake

Forgiving God, be with those who need to forgive themselves. May they know your love for them regardless of the situation.

Resentment

Dear God, please replace resentment with joy and contentment in the lives of those who are struggling.

Sadness

Healing God, be with those who experience sadness and surround them with the joy of your love.

Stress

O Lord, be with those who lives are overcome with stress.

Worry

O Lord, help all those whose lives are bound up and lost in constant worry to be able to put their trust in you.

Meeting Special Needs

Hebrews 12:1

Therefore, since we are surrounded by so great a cloud of witnesses, let us also lay aside every weight and the sin that clings so closely, and let us run with perseverance the race that is set before us.

Learn

Participants will learn about physical disabilities and create a game of "Go Fish" to suggest ways to respond to these situations.

Locate

- ► Bible
- ► Cards, 3" x 5"
- ► Chalk or marker
- ► Chalkboard or newsprint
- ► Markers or colored pencils (optional)
- ► Pens

Advance Preparation

- ► Write the following need statements on a chalkboard or newsprint:
  - ► Need: I have to work overtime and need someone to start supper.
  - ► Need: I need a ride to basketball practice.
  - ► Need: I need someone to help me move a piece of furniture.

Lead

Persons with physical or other disabilities can experience unique challenges as they undertake "running the race" of daily life. In many cases, taken-for-granted tasks meet with overwhelming obstacles. In this lesson, participants will learn about a variety of physical conditions and create a game of "Go Fish" to teach ways in which people can help persons with special needs to help themselves.

Begin the lesson by telling the class that everyone has needs that can be met by other people. Ask how group members help people in their families meet their personal needs. Direct attention to the statements written on the chalkboard or newsprint. Ask the students to suggest solutions to these situations.

For example:

- ► Need: I have to work overtime and need someone to start supper.
  Response: I will come home in time to start it.

- ► Need: I need a ride to basketball practice.
  Response: I can take you on my way to work.

- ► Need: I need someone to help me move a piece of furniture.
  Response: We can move it together.

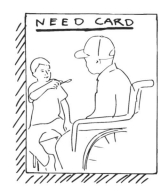

NEED CARD

RESPONSE CARD

Organize a schedule to help the boy at lunch.

NEED CARD

Wheelchair cannot fit through narrow school door.

RESPONSE CARD

Petition the school to reconstruct doorway for equal access.

After the students have suggested responses to these situations and others such as caring for a younger sibling, doing yard work, or sharing a new skill, tell them that individuals who are physically challenged have many needs that can, and must, be met by other people. Compile a list of challenging conditions. These could include autism, birth defects, blindness and visual impairments, cerebral palsy, cystic fibrous, deafness and hearing impairments, Down syndrome, emotional disturbance, intellectual disability, language or speech impairment, learning disabilities, mental retardation, orthopedic impairment, pediatric diabetes, and traumatic brain injury. Discuss any condition that needs further explanation. Point out that some people may suffer from any one of these, even if it is not apparent. Be sensitive that this may be the case with children in the group.

Tell the group that they will prepare and play a version of the game "Go Fish." State that this activity will help everyone explore the needs of persons who are living with disabilities and propose ways in which people can respond to their needs. Guide the students in making a deck of "Go Fish" playing cards.

Begin by forming small groups and have each of them pick one of the physical challenges from the list such as blindness and visual impairments. Tell the teams to think of people who live with the condition they selected and discuss their needs and possible responses to them. Provide index cards and pens. Instruct the groups to print the word "Need" on one side of each of five cards. On the opposite side of each card they are to print the physical challenge and one need a person with it would face. For example, I am blind and need to make an airplane trip. Tell them to prepare four additional cards for their physical challenge. On five more cards, have the game-makers print the word "Response" on one side of each card. On the opposite sides of those cards, they are to write a way to meet the situation. For example, Blindness and Visual

Impairment—I will call the airline to make special arrangements for your trip.

Additional examples include:

► Need: I have an artificial leg, but would like to drive a car.

Response: We can check into special controls for physically challenged drivers.

► Need: I'm being sent to a new school on Monday and don't know how to get my wheelchair on the bus.

Response: I will stay with you until you are on the bus.

► Need: I'm on a special diet and don't know if I can eat the school lunch.

Response: I will talk to the kitchen staff at the school and see what they can do for you.

Remind the students to make the game interesting and informative by writing many different needs and responses. Stress ways in which people are independent, yet interdependent. The cards may also be illustrated if time and interest allow.

When the preparation is completed, gather the students around a table and use the cards to play a game of "Go Fish." Shuffle each deck of cards—needs and responses. Place the need cards face down in a pile in the center of the table. Then distribute five response cards to each player. Place the remaining response cards, face down,

in a separate pile. One player, such as the youngest in the group, starts by picking a need card from the stack, reads it, and asks a second player for a response to that need. If the second player has a response, he or she must read it and then give that card to the first player. The first player now has a match and should place the two cards where all can see them. If the second player does not have a response card to match, player two says "Go Fish" and player one picks a card from the response pile.

For example:

► John: I am in a wheelchair and cannot reach items in my upper kitchen cabinets. Can you help me?

► Mary: Yes. I know of a "grabber" tool that will help you.

Mary turns her card over to John. John sets both cards on the table in front of him. Since John made a match with the person he asked, he may take another turn. If he did not make a match, he would pick a card from the pile. If it matches, he takes another turn. If it does not match, someone else takes a turn, for example, the person to the right of the one who started the game.

Continue the activity until all of the cards are used or a time limit has been reached. Emphasize that everyone wins when people help each other.

Creating Recipes for Healthy Living

1 Corinthians 6:19

Or do you not know that your body is a temple of the Holy Spirit within you, which you have from God, and that you are not your own?

Learn

Participants, primarily middle and high school students as well as adults, will discuss eating issues and compile a book of recipes for healthy living.

Locate

- ► Bible
- ► Binders or folders
- ► Chalk or marker
- ► Chalkboard or newsprint
- ► Copy machine or printer
- ► Glue or glue sticks
- ► Information on eating disorders
- ► Magazines or newspaper ads
- ► Markers
- ► Paper for copy machine or printer
- ► Pens
- ► Punch, 3 hole
- ► Resource sheet: "Recipes for Healthy Living"

Advance Preparation

- ► Gather reference materials on eating disorders from books, counselors, doctors, local organizations, and websites and set up a resource table for groups to use during the lesson.
- ► Arrange for a dietitian or a nutritionist, as well as a counselor, to participate in this lesson to be sure that the food addiction topics are addressed carefully and thoughtfully in the group sessions as well as during one-on-one discussions.
- ► Make a copy of the Recipes for Healthy Living resource sheet for each group.
- ► Arrange for someone to make copies of the completed resource sheets.

Lead

Many people of all ages experience an eating disorder or an unhealthy food-related problem at some point in their lives. Many young people struggle with food issues as they grow through adolescence and young adulthood. During this activity, students will compile a notebook with definitions of common food and diet problems and list the dangers each poses to a healthy lifestyle. They will also develop healthy recipes that are good for all.

Ask the students to define or describe an eating disorder or problem. If their responses are not accurate or complete, explain that an eating disorder is a pattern or habit which is potentially harmful to a person physically and emotionally. On a chalkboard or newsprint list the eating disorders the students were able to name.

Suggest others such as:

► Anorexia

► Bulimia

► Fad diets

► Manipulation of weight for sports teams

► Obesity

► Poor food choices

Read the passage from 1 Corinthians 6:19: "Do you not know that your body is a temple of the Holy Spirit within you, which you have from God, and that you are not your own?" Ask the group what this verse has to do with eating habits. Discuss how people who truly believe these words will treat their bodies.

Explain that the class will work together to compile a book of recipes for healthy living. Assign each student or small group one of the eating issues from the list on the board. Provide each group with a Recipes for Healthy Living resource sheet and pens. Refer to the area with reference materials on eating issues and explain how they can be used to find data for the activity.

Review the information to be complied:

► **Names**: Names of members of the group

► **Issue**: The specific issue addressed in the paper

► **Definition**: A one sentence definition of the diet problem or eating disorder

► **Dangers**: A list of dangers associated with the problem

► **Solutions**: Suggestions for possible solutions to the problem such as counseling, an intervention by family or friends, medical help, support groups, talking with a coach or a teacher

Instruct the teams to either select a scribe to fill out their form or to give each member a turn to write a section of the sheet. Remind them to print or write firmly and neatly as the sheets will be duplicated for distribution to everyone in the class.

As part of the solutions, instruct the students to list things a friend could do to help a friend who is having trouble in this area. This may include encourage, listen, pray, or tell a responsible adult.

When the work is completed, return to the large group. Allow each team to share their report. Discuss each issue as it is presented and ask for additional ideas from other participants. Encourage the presenters to add any important contributions to their worksheets. Collect the worksheets. Arrange for a leader to duplicate them while the participants discuss healthy eating options.

State that healthy eating should be a way of life for children, youth, and adults. Invite each group to consider three positive things everyone can do to keep their bodies physically fit. Offer a few examples such as limiting processed foods, sugar, and meals at fast food restaurants. Provide time for each group to compile a list. When everyone is finished, or after five minutes, ask volunteers to share their responses. Be sure ideas like eating fruits, vegetables, whole grains, and fish are mentioned. Arrange for a leader to compile the suggestions on a page that can be duplicated and added to their booklets.

After the presentations are complete and the sheets are duplicated, set up separate piles for each issue. Provide a three-hole punch or several if they are available. Direct the participants to the table with the duplicated work sheets. Allow each person to collate and punch the collection of pages.

Distribute a binder or report folder to each person and tell them to create a cover design for their resource book. Provide glue or glue sticks, markers, magazines, newspaper ads, and scissors. Suggest that they print a title such as Recipes for Healthy Living or words of their choice on the front and draw or glue pictures and words to illustrate the theme as well. The verse, 1 Corinthians 6:19, could be written on the front, back, or inside cover. When everyone is finished, invite them to share their titles and designs. Encourage them to keep their books for future reference on this important issue.

Recipes for Healthy Living

Names	Dangers

Issue	Solutions

Definition	Friend to Friend

Uplifting the Sick

James 5:14

Are any among you sick? They should call for the elders of the church and have them pray over them, anointing them with oil in the name of the Lord.

Learn

Participants will organize a prayer marathon to express care for someone involved in an accident or who has recently become ill.

Locate

- ▶ Baskets, 2
- ▶ Bible
- ▶ Bulletin board or casel
- ▶ Candles (optional)
- ▶ Copy machine or printer
- ▶ Flowers (optional)
- ▶ Matches (optional)
- ▶ Paper for copy machine or printer
- ▶ Pencils or pens
- ▶ Poster board
- ▶ Ribbon, green and yellow
- ▶ Resource sheet: "Prayer Marathon Checklist"
- ▶ Resource sheet: "Prayer Marathon Scripture Verses"
- ▶ Resource sheet: "Prayer Marathon Sign-up Poster"
- ▶ Scissors

Advance Preparation

- ▶ Decide on the person to pray for during the prayer marathon. It could be someone from the congregation or school who was involved in a severe accident or diagnosed with a serious illness, it might be a friend or relative of a member of the parish, or it could be an individual in the community.

- ▶ Contact the family of a person who was in an accident or is ill, informing them of the plan to hold a prayer marathon and receiving their permission to proceed. Assure them that all arrangements will be taken care of and that they will not have any responsibilities for the event.

- ▶ Make copies of the Prayer Marathon Checklist and the Prayer Marathon Scripture Verses resource sheets for the participants.

- ▶ Enlarge the Prayer Marathon Sign-up resource sheet and print it on poster board.

- ▶ Cut green and yellow ribbon into six inch pieces to be used as part of the prayer service and the marathon. Place each color in a separate basket.

Lead

People who are injured in an accident or diagnosed with a serious illness often experience a long period of recovery. The person, as well as family members, need physical, emotional, and spiritual support. These folks need to know that people care for them as they go through a myriad of difficult experiences related to this misfortune. Often, people in the congregation the family attends or classmates at the school where the person goes want to show support but feel helpless because they do not know what to do. This lesson will encourage the participants to reach out to someone who has experienced a serious accident or is ill. The group will organize and participate in a prayer marathon to express their care and to look to God for help on behalf of the person and the family.

Introduce the idea of a prayer marathon. Explain that this type of event is a meaningful way to express care for a person as well as for the family. It is also a powerful way to seek God's help in a difficult situation. Discuss the particular situation and the person and family for whom the group will be praying. Inform the participants of the person's condition and any specific needs.

Read James 5:13-14 to the group: Are any among you suffering? They should pray. Are any cheerful? They should sing songs of praise. Are any among you sick? They should call for the elders of the church and have them pray over them, anointing them with oil in the name of the Lord. Remind the group that since biblical times Christians have met together to pray for people in need.

Plan the prayer marathon, if the leader has not elected to do this ahead of time. Remind the group that the purpose of the activity is to invite people to pray for the person involved in the accident at specific times throughout the event.

Distribute copies of the Prayer Marathon Checklist resource sheet. Discuss the items on the list and make tentative plans for each component of the event.

Decide on a location and check to see if it is available on the desired date. The event could be held in a chapel or sanctuary of a church, a classroom or hall of a school, a building in the community, or in homes of the members or participants. Obtain guidelines, if necessary, for use of the space.

Choose and confirm a date. Decide how long the marathon will last and set the time. The duration can be a few hours; a morning, afternoon, or evening; a twenty-four hour period; or an entire weekend. In addition, an hour might be set apart at the beginning of the marathon to initiate the event at a community prayer service.

Prepare a prayer marathon poster which provides information on the person for whom the event will be held; the date, time, and location; and time slots marked in equal increments, such as fifteen or thirty minute segments, for people to pledge to pray at either the chosen site or in their own homes. Place the poster on an easel or bulletin board where a large number of people will see it and attach a pen or pencil for people to use to claim a time slot.

Advertise the event in bulletins and newsletters as well as via email and a website. Make announcements to groups and hand out fliers. Solicit participants and encourage people to sign up in the time slots on the poster. Invite group members to choose a time for their own prayer involvement.

Solicit church or school leaders to participate in the initial, or opening, community prayer service. Arrange for music and ask an accompanist, soloist, and/or group to be involved. If a dance or drama team is available, ask them to take part as well. Determine the roles the class members will play. They could write and offer the gathering prayer and lead a time of intercessory prayer for the needs of the person and all involved. A response to the petitions can be "Lord, hear our prayer." Select one of the scripture suggestions from the Prayer Marathon Scripture Verses handout to be read. Ask someone in the group to offer a reflection following the reading. Distribute verses to all who take part in the service and during the individual prayer segments. These passages can be read and reflected on during the course of the prayer marathon as people fulfill their pledge to pray for a specific amount of time.

Prepare the physical setting for the service and the marathon. If available, candles and flowers would enhance the environment where the gathering will take place. Put the baskets of ribbons at the entrances and arrange for people to hand them out. Explain that the ribbons may be used in several ways. The green ribbons represent life and the yellow ones stand for remembrance. The green ribbons can be placed on a table or altar in front of the church as part of each person's prayer for the life of the accident victim. They could also be tied to branches on a tree inside or outside the building. The yellow ribbons might be taken home to serve as a reminder to keep praying for the person. After the event the green ribbons can be collected in a basket and presented to the sick or injured person and the family.

The last step is to actually hold the event. Arrange for adult supervision during the hours of the marathon. In the midst of all of the preparations, remember to take time to pray. God will bless those who live out the words of James 5:13-14.

Prayer Marathon Checklist

Date

Determine the date of the event. Clear and confirm the day with the facility that will be used for the marathon.

Leadership

Recruit individuals or teams to be responsible for various aspects of the event.

Location

Decide on the location for the prayer marathon. It could be held at a church, school, community center, or in homes.

Program

Arrange for dancers, drama groups, and musicians to be part of the opening or closing service.

Publicity

Advertise the prayer marathon by placing a notice in forms of communication like the church bulletin, an email blast, a weekly or monthly newsletter, and a website.

Prepare a prayer marathon poster which gives information on the person for whom the event will be held as well as the date, time, and location. Include time slots for which people can sign up to pray.

Time

Set the time for the prayer marathon. It could be held for two to three hours; a morning, afternoon, or evening; a day; or an entire weekend. Include a communal prayer service to launch the event.

Prayer Marathon Scripture Verses

Psalm 23

The Lord is my shepherd, I shall not want. He makes me lie down in green pastures; he leads me beside still waters; he restores my soul. He leads me in right paths for his name's sake. Even though I walk through the darkest valley, I fear no evil; for you are with me; your rod and your staff - they comfort me. You prepare a table before me in the presence of my enemies; you anoint my head with oil; my cup overflows. Surely goodness and mercy shall follow me all the days of my life, and I shall dwell in the house of the Lord forever.

Psalm 46

God is our refuge and strength, a very present help in trouble. Therefore we will not fear, though the earth should change, though the mountains shake in the heart of the sea; though its waters roar and foam, though the mountains tremble with its tumult. There is a river whose streams make glad the city of God, the holy habitation of the Most High. God is in the midst of the city; it shall not be moved; God will help it when the morning dawns. The nations are in an uproar, the kingdoms totter; he utters his voice, the earth melts. The Lord of hosts is with us; the God of Jacob is our refuge. Come, behold the works of the Lord; see what desolations he has brought on the earth. He makes wars cease to the end of the earth; he breaks the bow, and shatters the spear; he burns the shields with fire.

'Be still, and know that I am God! I am exalted among the nations, I am exalted in the earth.' The Lord of hosts is with us; the God of Jacob is our refuge.

Psalm 103:1-5

Bless the Lord, O my soul, and all that is within me, bless his holy name. Bless the Lord, O my soul, and do not forget all his benefits - who forgives all your iniquity, who heals all your diseases, who redeems your life from the Pit, who crowns you with steadfast love and mercy, who satisfies you with good as long as you live so that your youth is renewed like the eagle's.

Psalm 118:4-5

Let those who fear the Lord say, 'His steadfast love endures forever.' Out of my distress I called on the Lord; the Lord answered me and set me in a broad place.

Psalm 139:7-14

Where can I go from your spirit? Or where can I flee from your presence? If I ascend to heaven, you are there; if I make my bed in Sheol, you are there. If I take the wings of the morning and settle at the farthest limits of the sea, even there your hand shall lead me, and your right hand shall hold me fast. If I say, 'Surely the darkness shall cover me, and the light around me become night,' even the darkness is not dark to you; the night is as bright as the day, for darkness is as light to you. For it was you who formed my inward parts; you knit me together in my mother's womb.

I praise you, for I am fearfully and wonderfully made. Wonderful are your works; that I know very well.

Isaiah 40:30-31

Even youths will faint and be weary, and the young will fall exhausted; but those who wait for the Lord shall renew their strength, they shall mount up with wings like eagles, they shall run and not be weary, they shall walk and not faint.

Isaiah 43:1-3a

But now thus says the Lord, he who created you, O Jacob, he who formed you, O Israel: Do not fear, for I have redeemed you; I have called you by name, you are mine. When you pass through the waters, I will be with you; and through the rivers, they shall not overwhelm you; when you walk through fire you shall not be burned, and the flame shall not consume you. For I am the Lord your God, the Holy One of Israel, your Savior. I give Egypt as your ransom, Ethiopia and Seba in exchange for you.

Jeremiah 29:11-13

For surely I know the plans I have for you, says the Lord, plans for your welfare and not for harm, to give you a future with hope. Then when you call upon me and come and pray to me, I will hear you. When you search for me, you will find me; if you seek me with all your heart.

Luke 4:18-21

'The Spirit of the Lord is upon me, because he has anointed me to bring good news to the poor. He has sent me to proclaim release to the captives and recovery of sight to the blind, to let the oppressed go free, to proclaim the year of the Lord's favor.' And he rolled up the scroll, gave it back to the attendant, and sat down. The eyes of all in the synagogue were fixed on him. Then he began to say to them, 'Today this scripture has been fulfilled in your hearing.'

Prayer Marathon Sign-up Poster

For: _____

Date: _____

Time: _____

Location: _____

Time Slots:

Proclaiming the Message

Psalm 100:5
For the Lord is good;
his steadfast love endures forever,
and his faithfulness to all generations.

Learn

Participants will consider healthy choices that impact unborn and newborn children and create paper tube rod puppets to share public service announcements to raise awareness about this topic.

Locate

- ▶ Bible
- ▶ Cotton, fake fur, or yarn
- ▶ Craft sticks
- ▶ Equipment to make recordings
- ▶ Examples of Public Service Announcements
- ▶ Fabric scraps
- ▶ Felt
- ▶ Glue
- ▶ Paper
- ▶ Pencils or pens
- ▶ Scissors
- ▶ Tubes, paper – various sizes

Advance Preparation

- ▶ Arrange for community resource persons to speak to the group about health choices that impact unborn and newborn children.
- ▶ Plan to condense the activities into one session or determine how to spread them out over several weeks

Lead

Some individuals suffer throughout their entire lives because of choices made by other people. Everyday there are babies born with conditions that affect them physically and emotionally. Often these infants are innocent victims who have been hurt by a choice made by one or both of their parents. Many times individuals decide to engage in certain types of behavior, such as using drugs or alcohol, even though they know the results will be harmful to their unborn and newborn children. Fortunately, in most cases, there is something that can be done to avert these conditions. Awareness and education are important factors in making decisions that affect self and others. Help the participants explore this theme by making and using paper tube rod puppets to deliver helpful and hopeful messages in the form of Public Service Announcements.

Introduce the lesson by stating that sometimes the choices people make affect more than just themselves. This is certainly true in the case of people who use alcohol, cocaine, heroin, or tobacco products and then have children. Newborns whose parents abuse alcohol may be born with fetal alcohol syndrome. Babies of heroin addicts come into the world addicted to the drug and go through a painful withdrawal process which frequently has severe side effects. Children of a parent or parents who use cocaine are often born prematurely and must struggle to survive. Unborn and newborn babies are also affected when people engage in behaviors that cause STDs, sexually transmitted diseases, or HIV, Human Immunodeficiency Virus, the infection that causes Acquired Immune Deficiency Syndrome, AIDS. STDs may cause a baby to be born blind or with visual handicaps and HIV infection results in an impaired immune system which causes severe health issues. In addition, if a pregnant girl or woman chooses to neglect pre-natal care or proper nutrition her decision can have a devastating effect on the innocent child.

Help the participants become aware of ways in which unhealthy choices related to substance abuse, sexual behavior, and lifestyle affect unborn and newborn babies. Invite community resource persons to share information with the class. Schedule a talk by one or more individuals, or arrange for a panel discussion, to address this theme. Speakers could include representatives of alcoholism councils, counseling centers, health departments, HIV and AIDS ministries, medical professions, and substance abuse organizations.

Use the information provided by the speakers to help the students write statements that educate and inform others of the results of certain types of behavior, especially on innocent children. Tell the group that they will be writing Public Service Announcements and that they will be constructing tube puppets to impart the information.

Introduce the topic of Public Service Announcements by asking if anyone knows what "PSA" means. Explain that PSAs are Public Service Announcements that are aired on radio and television stations. PSAs communicate messages to the listening and viewing audiences about important topics and upcoming events. Ask if anyone has ever seen or heard a PSA. Play an example, if possible. Challenge the participants to think of messages regarding the topic of healthy choices involving unborn and newborn children that should be communicated to their community. Invite individuals or small groups to pick one or several subjects, such as heroin addiction or lack of pre-natal care, and to write or record Public Service Announcements to use with their puppets. Write at least one example together, such: "Today's choices affect tomorrow's children," "Think about their future," or "When you drink, your baby drinks too." Distribute paper and pens or pencils to the students. Guide the group as they prepare the Public Service Announcements.

When the group has completed this part of the lesson, ask the participants to set their writing aside and to direct their attention to the procedure for making a puppet from a paper tube. Cylinders of any size, ranging from toilet tissue rolls, paper towel tubes, or wrapping paper cores, may be used for the project. Note that each person is to create a puppet representing him or her self to use to deliver the announcement.

Form the puppet face by cutting a piece of felt and gluing it to the top one-third of the tube. Make facial features from felt scraps and glue them in place. Yarn or fake fur becomes hair and should be attached to the top of the tube. Glue a piece of felt around the remainder of the tube to serve as the undergarment. Layers of fabric in contrasting or complementary colors can be added as over garments. Make arms from strips of cloth or felt and glue them to the sides of the tube. Apply a craft stick to the inside back of the tube to serve as the rod by which the puppet is operated.

If felt is not available, use construction paper instead. The facial features may be drawn on with marker. Substitute tissue paper for fabric to form the outer garments.

Provide the supplies for the puppet making project and guide the group as they construct their characters. Once the puppets are completed, take turns using them to make the public service announcements.

To extend the activity, have the students take turns recording their puppets delivering the Public Service Announcements. The final version could be sent to a radio or television station to air on their programs, posted to YouTube for others to view, or played at a church or school open house.

Remind the participants that the most effective Public Service Announcement is a lifestyle that involves healthy choices which impact their lives and the lives of others.

Ministering In Mercy

Matthew 5:7

'Blessed are the merciful, for they will receive mercy.'

Learn

Participants will research organizations that assist terminally ill children and create pennants to display information about their work.

Locate

▶ Bible

▶ Bulletin board

▶ Clothesline (optional)

▶ Clothes pins (optional)

▶ Computer with internet access

▶ Copy machine or printer

▶ Dowel rods

▶ Envelopes

▶ Fabric, felt, or paper

▶ Glue

▶ Markers, permanent

▶ Paper for copy machine or printer

▶ Pens

▶ Resource sheet: "Ministries of Mercy"

▶ Scissors

▶ Stamps

▶ Stationery

Advance Preparation

▶ Duplicate a copy of the Ministries of Mercy resource sheet for each participant.

Lead

There are many children who suffer from terminal illnesses. A terminal illness is one that leads to death; a disease or sickness for which there is no cure. Although it is disturbing to realize that there are many boys and girls who are seriously ill, it is also comforting to discover that help and hope is available for these young people and their families. Many organizations provide services to terminally ill children that embody the words of Jesus' beatitude "Blessed are the merciful." Use this activity to acquaint the participants with the purposes and programs of organizations that provide support and services to terminally ill children.

Explain that serious illnesses like cancer and leukemia affect children as well as adults. Emphasize that while it is distressing to think and to talk about children who may not get better, there are many sources of help for chronically ill children and their families.

Distribute copies of the Ministries of Mercy resource sheet. Acquaint the participants with the programs of various groups and share a brief explanation of each. Tell the participants that they will be contacting one of the groups to request more information about the services it provides. This activity will help the students discover and discuss some of the ways in which topics related to terminal illness may be addressed. Provide an overview of the ministry and mission of groups such as:

A Special Wish Foundation

Professionals work to grant wishes of children and adolescents under 21 years of age who are afflicted with a life-threatening disorder.

A Wish with Wings

Raises funds and makes arrangements with community groups to donate services or funding to make wishes of catastrophically ill children for toys, trips, or introductions to celebrities financially possible.

Children's Wish Foundation International

Seeks to fulfill the wishes of terminally ill children under 18 years old.

Dream Factory

Volunteers devoted to granting the dreams of chronically or critically ill children.

Famous Fone Friends

Arranges for a well-known actor, athlete, or other celebrity to call a sick child.

Friends of Karen

Provides financial and emotional support to children with life-threatening illnesses and to their families.

Give Kids the World

Individuals who work to provide a six-day, cost-free vacation for terminally ill children and their families at Walt Disney World and other entertainment complexes.

Make a Wish Foundation

Grants the wishes of children with life-threatening illnesses, thereby providing these children and their families with special memories and a welcome respite from the daily stress of their situation.

Ronald McDonald House

Provides housing and hospitality to families of hospitalized children.

Sunshine Foundation

Volunteers whose purpose is to fulfill the wishes of children who suffer from kidney disease, leukemia, or cancer.

Pass out paper and pens and ask each participant, or team, to write to one of the agencies requesting information on its policies, programs, and publications. Provide envelopes and postage and make sure that the letters are mailed. As an option, the participants may contact each group via their website and request the information.

In addition to the national organizations listed, contact local institutions and agencies such as children's hospitals, churches, counseling centers, funeral homes, hospice, and service groups to determine the support and services they provide.

When the materials arrive, invite the participants to make flag shaped banners, called pennants, to tell the stories of the groups they researched. By displaying the information in this way, everyone can learn about the diversity and focus of various groups.

Place the supplies for the project within sharing distance of the participants. Felt, fabric, or paper may be used for the background of the flags. Tell the banner-makers to cut the material into the shape of a flag or pennant. Remind the group that pennants are used to cheer on schools and sports teams. These pennants cheer on organizations which are ministering in mercy. Using permanent markers, have each person write the name and draw the logo of the group represented by the flag. As an alternative, this information may be cut from the literature and glued in place. Allow time for the group to design and decorate their flags with words and pictures that describe the mission of the organization they studied. Tape or glue a dowel rod to one side of each banner.

Display the completed flags on a bulletin board or a clothesline or use them in a parade or procession.

Ministries of Mercy

A Special Wish Foundation
Social workers, psychologists, physicians, nurses, business people, and attorneys who work to grant wishes of children and adolescents under 21 years of age who are afflicted with a life-threatening disorder.

1250 Memory Lane, Suite B
Columbus, OH 43209
614-258-3186
800-486-WISH
SpWish.org

A Wish with Wings
Raises funds and makes arrangements with community groups to donate services or funding to make wishes of catastrophically ill children for toys, trips, or introductions to celebrities financially possible.

3751 West Freeway
Fort Worth, TX 76107
(817) 469-9474
AWWW.org

Children's Wish Foundation International
Seeks to fulfill the wishes of terminally ill children under 18 years old.

8615 Roswell Road
Atlanta, GA 30358
800-323-WISH
ChildrensWish.org

Dream Factory
Volunteers devoted to granting the dreams of chronically or critically ill children.

410 W. Chestnut Street
Louisville, KY 40202
(502) 561-3001
800-456-7556
DreamFactoryInc.org

Famous Fone Friends
Arranges for a well-known actor, athlete, or other celebrity to call a sick child.

9101 Sawyer Street
Los Angeles, CA 90035
(310) 204-5683
FamousFoneFriends.org

Friends of Karen
Provides financial and emotional support to children with life-threatening illnesses and to their families.

118 Titicus Road
North Salem, NY 10560
(914) 277-4547
FriendsOfKaren.org

Give Kids the World
Individuals who work to provide a six-day, cost-free vacation for terminally ill children and their families at Walt Disney World and other entertainment complexes.

210 S. Bass Road
Kissimmee, FL 34746
(407) 396-1114
GKTW.org

Make a Wish Foundation
Grants the wishes of children with life-threatening illnesses, thereby providing these children and their families with special memories and a welcome respite from the daily stress of their situation.

1702 E. Highland Avenue, Suite 400
Phoenix, AZ 85016
(602) 279-9474
800-722-9474
Wish.org

Ronald McDonald House
Provides housing and hospitality to families of hospitalized children.

110 N. Carpenter Street
Chicago, IL 60607
630-623-7048
RMHC.org

Sunshine Foundation
Volunteers whose purpose is to fulfill the wishes of children who suffer from kidney disease, leukemia, or cancer.

101 Lakeside Park
Southampton, PA 18966
215-396-4770
SunshineFoundation.org

Taking Care of the Sick

Matthew 25:36b

'I was sick and you took care of me.'

Learn

Participants will create a pocket banner as a tool to assist people recovering from sickness and surgery.

Locate

- ▶ Bible
- ▶ Cards, 3" x 5"
- ▶ Chalk or marker
- ▶ Chalkboard or newsprint
- ▶ Dowel rod
- ▶ Fabric, calico or print, or felt
- ▶ Glue
- ▶ Labels, self-sticking
- ▶ Needles or sewing machine
- ▶ Pencil or pen
- ▶ Ribbon
- ▶ Ruler or tape measure
- ▶ Scissors
- ▶ String or yarn
- ▶ Thread

Advance Preparation

Choose a fabric, such as calico or felt, for the background of the banner. Cut a piece which is approximately three feet wide by four feet long. If using a woven fabric, turn over the edges, sewing them in place so that the material will have a finished edge which will not unravel. Turn one three foot side over one inch and stitch in place to form a casing for the dowel rod.

Lead

'I was sick and you took care of me,' Jesus' words in Matthew 25:36b, may seem like they are aimed at people in the medical profession. Rather, caring for the sick is an important ministry of all Christians. Expressions of care can take many forms. Often simply making contact with a person who is ill and offering encouragement is the best expression of care. In this activity, the participants will make a banner to remind individuals in their church or school of the needs of sick people in their community. Through the use of the banner the group will be able to stay informed about the needs which a sick person has and will be able to volunteer to help meet them.

Ask the students if any of them have had family members or friends who have experienced a long recovery from a sickness or a surgery. Remark that during a period of convalescing there are things people normally do for themselves that they cannot do while recuperating from the illness or operation. Ask what kind of help a person who is bedridden or homebound would need. The students might name things like babysitting young children, shopping for groceries, preparing meals, or driving to the doctor. Record the responses on a chalkboard or a piece of newsprint.

Read Matthew 25:36b, 'I was sick and you took care of me.' Ask if any of the participants have ever helped a person who was sick. Then ask how they knew what they could do to be helpful. Some answers could be, "Tessa lives next door and I could see the grass getting long," or, "Juan Carlos is a friend of my father's and my dad asked me to help." Tell the group that often people are willing to help the sick, but they don't know what is needed or how they might get involved. Also share that if everyone calls the sick person to ask what he or she needs, it will be difficult for that person to rest.

Invite the group to make a banner with many pockets to hang in the church or school. The pockets will be labeled with the names of people in need, using removable, replaceable self-sticking address labels. In this way the banner can be used on an on-going basis as new situations and opportunities arise. Each pocket will contain cards specifying the needs of the person recovering from sickness or surgery.

Since the pockets will be attached to the bottom of the banner, the group should create a design for the top one-third of the space. Brainstorm ideas that will convey the purpose of the banner. The design might

include the words of Matthew 25:36b. Cut the symbols and words out of fabric or felt and glue or stitch them in place.

The pockets for the banner should be four inches by four inches. If the backing is felt, they could be cut from a variety of colors which compliment the design of the banner. If using calico fabric, the pockets could be cut out of a variety of patterns, creating a patchwork appearance. Glue or stitch the pockets in place, spacing them evenly and decoratively along the bottom two-thirds of the banner. Label some of the pockets with the names of people who are in need of help.

Write the names and specific needs of sick people from the parish, school, or community on index cards and slip them into the pocket that is labeled with their name. When people are interested in helping they will read the need on a card and then sign their name if they agree to complete the suggested task. Remember to prepare a card for each person's pocket stating "Offer prayers" and one reading "Send a card," since both of these suggestions are ongoing needs for anyone who is ill. The index cards should be updated as new needs arise. Address labels can also be added or deleted as necessary.

When the project is completed, slide a dowel rod through the casing at the top of the banner. Tie the ribbon in place as a hanger. Attach a pen or pencil using ribbon, string, or yarn. Hang the banner in a location where it can be seen by many people and used as a tool to care for the sick.

Portraying Health Issues

Luke 10:34
He went to him and bandaged his wounds, having poured oil and wine on them. Then he put him on his own animal, brought him to an inn, and took care of him.

Learn

Participants will create a word web of responses to the phrase "Health Care" and use the data to develop a cooperative cartoon illustrating the themes.

Locate

- ► Bible
- ► Chalkboard or newsprint
- ► Chalk or marker
- ► Markers
- ► Pencils or pens
- ► Paper, 8 ½" x 11"
- ► Tape

Lead

In a familiar parable, recorded in Luke 10:25-37, a Samaritan provides care for a traveler attacked by robbers on his way from Jerusalem to Jericho. Not only did the Samaritan bring the injured individual to a place where he could receive treatment, the man also paid for the care out of his own pocket. In today's society, health care issues are a compelling concern. For many people, access to adequate health care is limited by the high cost of insurance and co-pays, or the availability of adequate supplies and equipment. Explore the subject of health care through a word web and portray some of the issues in the form of a cooperative cartoon.

Addressing issues concerning health care is a cooperative matter. Many of the themes and topics related to the subject are common in all 50 states. Tell the group that they will explore health care issues by asking members of the congregation to respond to the words—Health Care—and printing their responses around the original phrase in a manner called a word web. Distribute paper and markers. Ask the group to print - Health Care - in bold block capital letters in the center of their paper.

State the guidelines for the activity. Tell the group that they will be stationed in the entryway of the church before and after each service. They are to show the word on their paper—Health Care—and ask as many individuals as possible to say the first thing that comes to mind when they hear it or see it. The students are to record the responses anywhere on their paper, scattered around the phase in the center of the sheet. State if the participants will work alone or in small groups, and form teams, if necessary. Clarify the directions and answer questions. Allow time for this portion of the activity.

Once the word webs are completed, ask the participants to share the results. On a chalkboard or a piece of newsprint, record some of the findings. Common themes might involve access, cost, employee/employer benefits, hospitals, insurance, legislation, medicaid, medicare, and prescription drugs. Make sure that everyone understands the meaning of each term as it is mentioned.

Tell the class that they will use their findings, the words written on the board, to develop individual frames of a cooperative cartoon. As a way to unify the separate sections of the strip, challenge the group to create a cartoon character to include on each person's page. Post a sheet of newsprint, offer markers,

and involve each participant in the process of drawing the cartoon figure. Invite one person to draw the face, another the body, someone else the eyes, and so forth until each participant has taken a turn and the illustration is completed. Distribute paper and pens, pencils, and markers to the group. Direct each participant to select one theme and use it, as well as the cartoon character, to illustrate the selected topic. Everyone will draw his or her idea on a full sheet of paper. Note that the individual papers will be joined together to make the frames of a continuous cartoon strip.

As the students finish their "frames," tape the sections to the wall in a long, horizontal strip. When the entire cartoon is completed, ask each participant to stand by his or her drawing. Go down the line and invite the artists to describe what they drew, as well as to share any information and insight they gained to address health care issues.

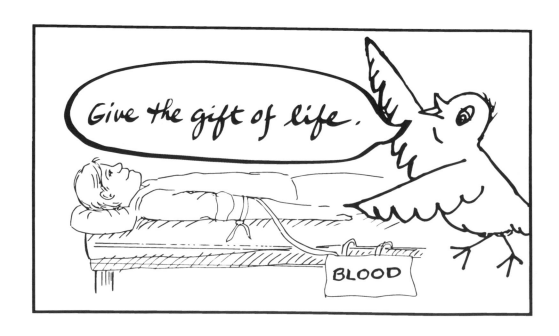

I WAS IMPRISONED

Jesus' directive in Matthew 25:36 to visit the imprisoned can be a difficult one for Christians. In order to live out this challenge, the understanding of what it means to be confined must be expanded. There are many ways to be or to feel imprisoned. While few people come into contact with people who are actually in detention centers or jail, everyone has daily encounters with people who are restricted in visible, as well as invisible, ways.

Painful experiences - for example, any form of emotional, mental, or physical abuse—can remain locked inside a person and become a form of imprisonment. Aging or poor health may cause problems which make people feel trapped in their own bodies or homes. Addiction to alcohol and drugs take away the freedom to make healthy and wise choices. Through intervention some people may be released from these situations while others cannot be freed, but still can feel the love and care of God through Christians who reach out to them in Jesus' name.

In this chapter, the more common daily experiences of imprisonment will be introduced. Activities in the ten lessons suggest ways for meeting the needs of those imprisoned with compassion and care. Following the lessons, participants will be better able to minister to the imprisoned they encounter in their families, friendship groups, schools, and faith communities. With the help of God, each participant will be equipped to say with the writer of Isaiah 61:1:

The Spirit of the Lord God is upon me, because the Lord has anointed me; [God] has sent me to bring good news to the oppressed, to bind up the brokenhearted, to proclaim liberty to the captives, and release to the prisoners.

Chart

Title	Scripture	Theme	Activity/Method	Page
Overview	▶ Isaiah 61:1 ▶ Matthew 25:36c, 39b, 43c, 44a	▶ Imprisoned		183
Spreading Some Sunshine	▶ Hebrews 13:3	▶ Families of Imprisoned	▶ Art: Sun/Rays Poster	185
Suffering for Their Beliefs	▶ Matthew 5:10-12 ▶ Acts 16:16-40 ▶ Philippians 1:12-13	▶ Persecution for Beliefs	▶ Creative Writing: Letters ▶ Storytelling: Biographies	187
Breaking Down Walls	▶ Ephesians 2:14	▶ Walls: Negative/ Positive Factors	▶ Architecture: Building Up and Breaking Down Walls	189
Overcoming the Bonds of Materialism	▶ Luke 12:34	▶ Consumer Messages ▶ Materialism	▶ Art: Collage – Advertisements and Alternatives ▶ Game: Maze/Obstacle Course	191
Learning about Literacy	▶ Ecclesiastes 4:14	▶ Literacy	▶ Game: Scrambled Words ▶ Music: Song to "Row, Row, Row Your Boat"	193
Unlocking the Fears	▶ Psalm 107:10	▶ Crime	▶ Game: Concentration – Crime Fighters ▶ Photography: Pictures – Items/ Crimes	197
Hiding in a Secret Prison	▶ Psalm 46:1	▶ Elderly Imprisonment	▶ Puppetry: Soft Sculpture Rod Puppet	199
Reading about Addictions	▶ Psalm 142:7	▶ Addiction	▶ Storytelling: Read-a-Thon Books and Resources	202
Touching with Love	▶ Matthew 8:3 ▶ Matthew 8:15 ▶ Mark 5:41 ▶ Mark 10:16 ▶ John 9:6	▶ Physical, Mental, and Emotional Imprisonment ▶ Healing Touch	▶ Dance/Gesture/Movement: Gestural Interpretation ▶ Music: "By Your Touch"; "Healing Hands" ▶ Photography: Hands	205
Feeling Trapped by Abuse	▶ Zechariah 9:12	▶ Abuse	▶ Banners/Textiles: Weaving	208

Spreading Some Sunshine

Hebrews 13:3

Remember those who are in prison, as though you were in prison with them; those who are being tortured, as though you yourselves were being tortured.

Learn

Participants will discover challenges faced by families of the imprisoned and consider ways to assist in some of these situations.

Locate

- ▶ Bible
- ▶ Chalk, black and bright colors including gold, orange, and yellow
- ▶ Markers, black, gold, orange, and yellow
- ▶ Poster board, 2' x 3'

Advance Preparation

Look on the internet or talk to the pastor or social justice committee to discover prison ministry or prisoner family support groups operating in the area. Contact these organizations about ways that the church or school might be able to assist in their work.

Lead

In the Gospels, Jesus challenges Christians to be mindful of people who have been convicted of crimes and are in institutions for punishment or rehabilitation. In addition, it is important to remember the families of people who are imprisoned. Families, often through no fault of their own, suffer because of lack of income, legal fees, and loneliness as well as the judgment, reactions, and stereotypes of others. Family members can become trapped by anger, guilt, or shame. In this lesson, the students will discuss ways to bring sunshine into the gray and cloudy lives of these families as they create a large sun poster depicting rays of help and hope.

Read Hebrews 13:3a to the group, "Remember those who are in prison, as though you were in prison with them." Ask if any of the participants remember those in prison. Most likely, people don't think about people in prison and if they do their thoughts are often associated with fear. Point out that group members probably think of the families of people in jail even less. Ask the group what happens to a person's family when he or she is sent to jail. In some ways they also become imprisoned by the things they experience and by the ways in which they are treated by others. This discussion should include the ideas given in the introduction, as well as issues like being forced to move, living without one parent, being placed in foster care, having negative feelings about oneself, and feeling sad.

On a piece of poster board, print words or phrases that name problems families face when a member is in prison. Write each word across the page in a straight line. If there is extra space left after the word, draw a line to the side of the page. Leave space between each line. When the list is complete, turn the poster on its side and note that the words and lines form the impression of jail bars on the paper.

Next use shades of gold, orange, and yellow chalk to draw circles in the middle of the poster board that overlap the design and form the center of a sun depiction. Add sun rays using the markers. Allow each participant an opportunity to help with the drawing. Then, ask what Christians can do to spread some sunshine into the lives of people with family members who are in prison.

On each ray take turns writing in marker one thing which people can do for the families of people who are in prison. Allow group members to suggest as many ideas as possible. These may include: acting kindly, being accepting, collecting school supplies, doing holiday activities, giving rides, helping with child care, inviting a speaker to provide information, listening to concerns, making donations to groups that help families, offering friendship, participating in an Angel Tree project, praying for family members, providing counseling services, remembering birthdays, sharing clothing.

Once the poster is completed, have the students choose a caption and write it on the artwork. Display the poster in a place where others will see it. This will help people to become more aware of the requirement of discipleship and of ways to enact it. If possible, put a note in a bulletin or newsletter to let people know about the project and the location of the display.

Suffering for Their Beliefs

Philippians 1:12-13

I want you to know, beloved that what has happened to me has actually helped to spread the gospel, so that it has become known throughout the whole imperial guard and to everyone else that my imprisonment is for Christ.

Learn

Participants will learn about men and women persecuted for their beliefs and compose letters to express the feelings of people in these situations.

Locate

- Bibles
- Paper
- Pencils or pens
- Reference materials about people persecuted for their beliefs

Advance Preparation

- Locate resource materials about people imprisoned or persecuted because of their beliefs.
- Research organizations with whom the group letter could be shared including Amnesty International:

Amnesty International USA
5 Penn Plaza, 16th Floor
New York, NY 10001, 212-807-8400
www.amnestyusa.org.

Lead

Philippians, a New Testament letter of Paul, is referred to as one of the prison letters because it is traditionally believed to have been written while Paul was imprisoned at Caesarea (AD 56-58) or in Rome (AD 61 to 63). Suffering for a right cause is one of the defining characteristics of Christian discipleship. Often the one who suffers will become an inspiration to others who hear about the suffering. Letters from the imprisoned to friends—as in the case of Saint Paul - link the person's suffering and the issue for which he or he is being persecuted to others. Letters of encouragement from friends and family to the person who is imprisoned can help him or her to better endure the experience. In this activity the students will learn about people imprisoned for their beliefs and compose letters to express the feelings of individuals in these situations.

Distribute Bibles to the students and read Matthew 5:10-12 together: 'Blessed are those who are persecuted for righteousness' sake, for theirs is the kingdom of heaven. Blessed are you when people revile you and persecute you and utter all kinds of evil against you falsely on my account. Rejoice and be glad, for your reward is great in heaven, for in the same way they persecuted the prophets who were before you.' Respond to the words of the verse with surprise at phrases and words like "be glad, blessed, and rejoice." Express wonder at how these words can be associated with persecution, pain, and suffering.

Next, organize the class into four groups. Assign each team a chapter from the book of Philippians. Remind the students that these words were written by Paul while he was in prison for his Christian beliefs. Provide paper and pencils or pens. Ask the students to read their chapter and to write down descriptions of what Paul experienced, a list of feelings he had, and words of encouragement he offered. When ready, ask one person from each group to summarize the discussion and to share one or two points with the large group. Conclude by asking if Paul's messages were expected and if any of his words were surprising. The story of Paul and Silas found in Acts 16:16-40 is another example. If there is time, read the passage.

Share that amazing things can happen, even in prison, by the power of God. State that there are many people who have experienced miraculous, unusual, and life-changing things while imprisoned or during times of persecution. Letters and diaries from these people have encouraged countless others throughout time. Their stories are amazing, uplifting and even blessed. Biblical characters such as Daniel, Peter, John, Paul, and Stephen experienced persecution. Historical figures include Polycarp, Joan of Arc, Dietrich Bonhoeffer, Martin Luther King, Jr., Anne Frank, and Corrie Ten Boom. Many contemporary people suffered and died for their beliefs such as: Jean Donovan; Archbishop Oscar Romero; Christian converts in Chiapas, Mexico; Nelson Mandela; Eastern European Christians; and protesters in Tienanmen Square. Many nuns, priests, pastors, and missionaries have given their lives helping "the least of these" in countries around the world. If available, distribute materials about some of the people

listed and others. Allow time for the students to review the information in books and on internet sites.

Give an overview of the ministry of Amnesty International, a group that works to free prisoners of conscience around the word. If available, distribute materials about some of these people to each group. Then ask the participants to imagine that they have been imprisoned because of something they believe. Instruct each person or group to write a letter expressing their feelings about being in prison and about being persecuted for what they believe. Provide paper and pencils and pens. Allow time for reflection and writing, offering assistance and encouragement as needed. When the project is completed, share the letters with others in the small group.

To extend the activity, compose a group letter for someone who is imprisoned unfairly for his or her beliefs. This letter should include messages of encouragement and care. Perhaps some phrases from Paul's writings to the Philippians, studied earlier, could be included. Make sure each person contributes at least one sentence or idea to the letter. When it is complete, re-read the letter one more time, adding any ideas which are helpful. Share the letter with others by submitting a copy to Amnesty International to include in their newsletter.

Conclude the lesson by re-reading Matthew 5:10-12 or Philippians 1:12-13 to or with the group. Offer a prayer thanking God for the witness of people who, throughout time, have been persecuted for their beliefs and ask God for courage today to hold firm to Christian convictions regardless of the circumstances and the consequences.

Breaking Down Walls

Ephesians 2:14

For he is our peace; in his flesh he has made both groups into one and has broken down the dividing wall, that is, the hostility between us.

Learn

Participants will demonstrate factors that build up and break down walls between people.

Locate

▶ Bibles

▶ Brushes, paint

▶ Cardboard bricks, cartons, or shoe boxes

▶ Crayons or markers

▶ Glue or tape

▶ Magazines

▶ Newspaper

▶ Newsprint, brown paper grocery bags, or poster paint

▶ Scissors

Lead

There are many types of cultural, economic, political, religious, and social walls that imprison or separate individuals and groups from one another. Tangible signs of barriers are evident in forms such as boundary walls and electrified fences. Intangible indications of walls include divisions based on economics, language, and race. In this activity, participants will use Ephesians 2:14 as a guide to discover some of the factors involved in building walls between people, as well as actions necessary to break them down. Learners will be challenged to realize that each person has the ability and the power to do away with the barriers that separate individuals and groups and to build positive pathways or bridges between people.

Read Ephesians 2:14 as an introduction to the theme. Ask the participants to list some of the negative emotions that build walls between people. Use a marker to print these ideas in one column on a piece of newsprint. Examples could include anger, fear, greed, hate, jealousy, and prejudice. Then, in a corresponding column, list positive values that break down these walls such as acceptance, cooperation, love, openness, sharing, and understanding.

Tell the students that they will be building a wall of negative emotions and also discovering ways to break down the wall through positive actions and attitudes. Direct each participant to choose a negative and a positive value from the list to use for the activity. Distribute one cardboard brick, box, or carton to each pupil. Provide materials such as paint, brushes, paper, glue, tape, magazines, newspapers, and scissors. Instruct the learners to cover their boxes with paper or paint. Ask each person to print the positive and the negative word on opposite sides of his or her brick. Additional descriptive words and pictures may be written or drawn on the sides, or cut from newspapers and magazines and glued in place.

After the bricks have been completed, have the students construct a wall of negative emotions by aligning the blocks so that the negative sides of the bricks face the same direction. As each piece is put in place, ask the participants to cite an example or discuss a situation of how the emotion described by the word influences people in various parts of the world. For example, people lose jobs because of fear of other employees; families reject relatives because of hurt and anger; immigration laws are stricter for people from certain countries or for those with various illnesses. When everyone has added a negative brick, allow each person to symbolically knock down part of the wall. Point out the role each individual plays in changing attitudes toward other people.

Finally, have the group take the scattered bricks and build a pathway of positive values. The bricks will form the border of the path and the positive values should be face up. Invite the group to walk through the pathway. Have each person pick up his or her block. Suggest that they keep their pieces as reminders to work toward breaking down the attitudes and actions that imprison or separate people or groups from one another. Gather the group in a circle and close the activity with a prayer asking God to prepare each participant to be a bridge to peace.

Overcoming the Bonds of Materialism

Luke 12:34
For where your treasure is, there your heart will be also.

Learn

Participants will consider a maze of consumer messages and discover alternatives to being trapped by material possessions.

Locate

► Bible
► Glue, dots or sticks
► Magazines
► Markers
► Newsprint
► Paper, 11" x 17" or larger
► Pens
► Tape, masking

Advance Preparation

► With masking tape, mark a maze pattern on the floor of the meeting space. Use walls and things like bulletin boards, boxes, chairs, desks, easels, or other furniture to form "road blocks" or "dead ends." The dead ends serve two purposes: actual stops along the way and places where individual collages the students make can be hung. Place a blank piece of 11" x 17" paper, as well as markers and pens, at each of the dead ends.

Lead

The "bonds of materialism" is a way to describe how a person can be a servant to his or her possessions and to the desire to have even more things. Many people gauge their happiness according to the cost, size, and style of items like cars, clothes, electronics, and homes. A person can become trapped in a life where what is important is what he

or she owns or hopes to be able to obtain. Oppositely, Jesus told his disciples to work for inexhaustible heavenly treasure, the kind that "no thief comes near and no moth destroys" (Luke 12:33). In this activity the participants will move through a maze to remind them how easy it is to get lost in the trap of consumer messages which surround people in today's society. They will also make collages depicting material obsessions which entrap people and offer alternative ideas to help people avoid this form of imprisonment.

Introduce the topic by talking about possessions which people want and which advertisers work hard to sell. As the participants name items, record the words on newsprint. Write fairly large, scattering the words around the page, to create a chaotic appearance. Mention how overwhelming advertising messages can be. Ask questions like: How have you been influenced to buy something you've seen in an ad or a commercial? Why do companies pour billions of dollars into advertising each year?

Point out that businesses advertise in order to feed on people's desire to have things. In a way, they understand what it says in Luke 12:34, "For where your treasure is there your heart will be also." Define materialism as the belief "that comfort, pleasure, and wealth are the only or highest goals or values to be attained." Materialism is a trap in which people can easily become captured. Ask the group to talk about why that is true. They may mention things such as becoming imprisoned by debt in order to get something a person wants or using all of their time and energy earning money to buy things.

Assign each individual, pair, or small group to make a collage that focuses on one of the material things that people desire. Assign or have the students choose items from the list such as: beauty products/cosmetics; cars/jeeps/trucks; clothes; electronics; gadgets and the latest products; houses; music; recreation; travel/vacations. Distribute magazines, glue sticks or tape, and background paper. Pictures and words may be cut from the materials provided or drawn and written on the collage. When the posters are completed, have the students tape their collages on one of the "dead ends" of the maze. Take time to clean up the art supplies before proceeding with the lesson.

Prepare individuals or pairs to go through the maze. Remind everyone that materialism, the desire to have things, can imprison people. Emphasize, however, that there are ways to escape the trap. People can live happily without or with fewer of the things advertisers tell them they must have. Explain to the learners that wherever they find a collage in the maze, it is a dead end where they must stop. In order to get around that trap, they must write an alternative way of living on the paper hanging next to the collage. For example, alternatives to the vehicles collage may include ideas like buying a used car, carpooling, and using public transportation. Remind everyone that they don't only have to suggest ways to live without the items, they can also offer ways to feel comfortable with less of a particular product. For example, they do not have to give up buying beauty or personal care items, but they might choose less expensive brands or set a monthly budget for themselves. Also, as the players consider alternatives, encourage them to think of ideas that are not already on the list.

After everyone has gone through the maze, sit down as a group. Collect the collages and the posters of alternative suggestions. Discuss the ideas, adding any that were not included. Then invite volunteers to cut the collages into pieces and distribute the sections to the participants. Offer pens and ask the students to write on the back of their piece one way an item can imprison them and one alternative choice they can make to be free of its control. Encourage everyone to take the papers home and to place them somewhere relevant to the message such as in their clothes closet, on the bathroom mirror, or in the car. Read the verse, Luke 12:34, and challenge the group to seek heavenly treasure over earthly treasure.

Learning about Literacy

Ecclesiastes 4:14
One can indeed come out of prison to reign, even though born poor in the kingdom.

Learn

Participants will play a game of scrambled words to discover ways illiteracy imprisons people.

Locate

► Bible
► Cards, 3" x 5"
► Copy machine or printer
► Markers
► Newsprint
► Paper for copy machine or printer
► Pencils or pens
► Resource sheet: "Scrambled Words"
► Statistics on illiteracy

Advance Preparation

► Duplicate one copy of the Scrambled Words resource sheet for each participant.
► Obtain current statistics on illiteracy from an internet source or from a Literacy Council.
► Print each letter of the word "I L L I T E R A C Y" on a separate 3" x 5" card.

Lead

Surprisingly, a high percentage of adults in the United States are illiterate. Although this means that some people cannot read or write at all, this statistic more accurately represents the number of people who read at the level of a grade school child. Because of the inability to read, or to comprehend what is read, people are imprisoned in numerous ways. Many non-readers are unemployed, or underemployed, because they do not have the basic skills to fill out an application or to hold a job. Most illiterate people live at the poverty level; in fact the number of functionally illiterate adults corresponds to the number of people living within this income bracket. Since illiterate people cannot read driver's tests, street signs, or maps, their mobility is limited. In this learning experience participants will explore information about one form of imprisonment, illiteracy, through the use of a word game and a song writing activity.

Before explaining the theme of the session, distribute an index card containing one letter of the word illiteracy to ten different people. Challenge the ten people to look at the letters on the cards and to use them to spell one word. If the group is able to solve the problem, have them stand in a line and display the letters in the correct sequence. If they are unable to unscramble and spell the word, point out that this is how many illiterate people—individuals who cannot read or who have difficulty reading—feel when they look at words.

Once the word is formed, ask someone to pronounce it. Also invite people to suggest definitions of the term. State that illiteracy is the inability to read and write. Functional illiteracy is the inability to read, write, and compute well enough to perform everyday tasks such as reading the directions on a medicine bottle or a recipe. When a person is illiterate it means that he or she is imprisoned in numerous ways. Ask the group to offer examples of how an illiterate person is imprisoned. Allow time for discussion and record the responses on a piece of newsprint. Explore ways in which the inability to read, or reading at the level of a grade school child, limits people. Distribute the list of scrambled words, and pencils or pens, and invite the learners to work individually or in small groups to decipher them. Explain that each word or phrase on the list is an item which presents a problem for a person who does not read well. Guide the group as they work on the project, offering encouragement and praise as needed.

After an appropriate amount of time, review the responses. For each answer ask the group to suggest ways the situation imprisons illiterate people. For example, someone who cannot read the directions on a prescription may take or give the wrong medicine. A low-level reader might not receive money from an insurance claim because the form was too hard to read and fill out. Job opportunities could be ignored because of the inability to read the want ads.

The answers to the scrambled words are:

1. Medicine bottle directions
2. Insurance form instructions
3. Children's bedtime stories
4. Street signs
5. Maps
6. Job applications
7. Want ads
8. Recipes
9. Menus
10. The Bible
11. Bank deposit slips
12. Bills
13. Letters
14. Assembly directions
15. Books
16. Admission forms
17. Greeting cards
18. Bus schedules
19. Advertisements
20. Newspapers.

Continue this discussion by introducing local, national, and international statistics on illiteracy rates. At present, the United States Department of Education estimates that 32 million, 14 percent, of the people living in the U.S.A. are illiterate and that 21 percent read below a fifth grade level. Worldwide, the illiteracy rate is 17 percent of the population. Expand the discussion by commenting on some of the causes of illiteracy such as learning disabilities, cycle of poverty, and school drop-outs.

Enhance this learning experience by inviting the participants to write songs exploring ways in which the issue of illiteracy can be addressed. Invite small groups to choose one item off of the word list, such as medicine bottle directions, and to write new words to a familiar tune suggesting ways in which a person could be helped with this task. Using the tune, "Row, Row, Row Your Boat," sing through the song one or two times and then show the students new words, such as:

Reading medicine bottle labels
is easier to do
if the doctor takes the time
to explain the directions to you.

Arrange the students into groups of four, provide newsprint and markers, and instruct them to use the same tune to write a new verse on the theme of improving literacy. Have each group share their song with the other learners. Encourage the pupils to work towards making the ideas expressed in the songs become reality.

Scrambled Words

Unscramble each word or phrase to learn a different way in which a person who is illiterate is imprisoned. Illiterate people cannot read:

1. cniedemi teotlb tenidsocri

2. unisanrec rfmo ttrssuiicnno

3. sedicnrlh metibde rsostei

4. tester nsgsi

5. pmas

6. bjo ltspaincpiao

7. tawn sad

8. csipree

9. nseum

10. eht lbibe

11. aknb pstioie spsil

12. slbli

13. treslet

14. msblysae tosrdcinie

15. kosbo

16. sndaiosmi rsfom

17. egrtgeni dacsr

18. ubs elsecuehs

19. tsdetirvmeanse

20. psenwpeasr

Unlocking the Fears

Psalm 107:10
Some sat in darkness and in gloom, prisoners in misery and in irons.

Learn

Participants will use photographs in a concentration game to explore ways that crime imprisons people and to suggest solutions.

Locate

- Bible
- Chalk
- Chalkboard or newsprint
- Data on crime in the United States
- Equipment to obtain photos such as cameras, computer and printer, magazines, newspapers, phones
- Glue
- Markers
- Paper, 8 1/2" x 11"
- Scissors

Advance Preparation

- Determine how photos of items symbolic of imprisonment through crime will be obtained. Two identical pictures are required for each theme. Options include: cut photos from magazines and newspapers; find copyright-free clip art or pictures on the internet and print two of each; draw two illustrations of each item on the list; organize a field trip to photograph examples. Allow time to obtain two shots of each photo.
- Prepare the concentration game. If necessary, glue each photo to a background sheet such as an 8 1/2" x 11" piece of paper. Two identical cards are needed for each example. If there are a large number of participants, prepare two or more games. Be sure to keep the pairs together within a given game.

Lead

According to the Federal Bureau of Investigation, the FBI, a violent crime or a property crime such as assault, burglary, murder, rape, or theft is committed in the U.S. every two seconds. Figures like these have forced people to become imprisoned in numerous ways. Men and women live in locked houses, afraid to attend evening events because of what might happen if they go out. Business owners guard their property by placing metal bars over windows and iron grates over doors. Drivers lock their car doors and use devices to deter auto theft. Women carry whistles or alarms to prevent attack. Travelers at airports are inconvenienced by metal detectors and security screenings. Crime imprisons people every day. Although this is a depressing subject and a deplorable situation, it is one that must be addressed. Exploration of this subject, however, can be done in creative and concrete ways.

Tell the group that they will use photography to consider the theme of imprisonment through crime and will also discover ways to empower people to respond with effective actions.

If appropriate, share current statistics available online from sources including the United States Department of Justice. Begin by asking for volunteers to raise their hands if they have ever: secured their home, locked their car doors, walked through a metal detector, seen a barbed wire fence, or noticed bars over a window or door of a business. Suggest that evidence of imprisonment to crime is all around us. Ask the group to brainstorm a list of examples and record the responses on a chalkboard or newsprint. Answers might include: barbed wire; fences; locked cars; home, business, and car security systems; gates; metal shutters; devices on steering wheels; bars on windows; metal detectors in public buildings, schools, and airports; security guards; signs and decals indicating protection services. Distribute or prepare two photo cards for the items on the list.

Tell the group that they will be using the pictures to play "Crime Fighters," a form of the game concentration. Shuffle the papers and lay them out, picture side down, in a tiled pattern on the floor or a table or hang them on a wall. Organize the group into two teams. Players from each team will alternate choosing two papers and turning them over. Explain that each time a match is made, the player will share one way to be a "Crime Fighter" and suggest ideas to address this issue. For example, if the picture of a locked car appears, the player might propose an escort or pick-up service for the elderly. A response to a picture of bars on windows or gates on doors could be to establish a neighborhood crime watch. For the illustration of metal detectors at schools, an educational program on safety could be offered. Encourage suggestions from the entire group if additional prompts are needed. Play the game in the following way. Each player may turn two cards over during his or her turn. If they match, another turn may be taken. If they do not match, the cards are returned to a face-down position. Then the next person attempts to make a match by turning over two cards. Play continues until all pairs have been uncovered and all topics have been discussed.

When the game is over, use the pictures as a bulletin board display. Provide paper and markers and invite the participants to add their "Crime Fighter" suggestions to the photos.

Hiding in a Secret Prison

Psalm 46:1
God is our refuge and strength, a very present help in trouble.

Learn

Participants will create soft sculpture rod puppets to explore ways in which elderly people can be imprisoned.

Locate

► Bible

► Cardboard tubes, paper towel size

► Crayons, make up, or markers in flesh tones

► Fabric pieces, various colors and sizes

► Fiberfill

► Foam rubber, 8"-10" x 1 1/2" pieces

► Glue, fabric or tacky

► Knife, utility type

► Material for hair such as cotton, fake fur, or yarn

► Needles

► Pantyhose or nylon stockings

► Pins, straight

► Puppet Stage

► Scissors

► Thread, colors to match stockings

Advance Preparation

► Launder the nylon stockings or pantyhose and cut them into 8" lengths.

► Set up a puppet stage in the activity area. If a stage is not available, use a doorway or a large appliance box to create one in advance or with the students. If using a door, block off the lower part with cardboard, heavy paper, or a table. Tape paper, fabric, or cord in strips in the opening to create bars, as in a jail cell. If using a large box, cut out one side to form an opening for the puppeteers. Cut out the upper portion of the opposite side of the box to make an opening for the puppets. In the stage opening, create the look of a window with bars.

Lead

Elderly people may feel imprisoned for many reasons. Physical changes, such as loss of hearing or sight or limited mobility, can separate an older person from full participation with others. Poverty or a fixed income can keep a person from doing favorite activities. Fear of crime can trap a man or woman inside their home. Some elderly people may feel confined in a nursing home where they do not choose to live. In this learning activity the group will discover ways in which elderly people may experience imprisonment and make soft sculpture puppets to enact some of these situations.

Begin the activity by asking the participants how elderly people might feel like prisoners or live lives of captivity. Invite the participants to brainstorm a list of examples which might include: loss of sight and hearing, physical ailments, living in an unsafe neighborhood, loss of a driver's license, and the death of a companion or a spouse. Also note that it is difficult for people with wonderful minds to feel confined by what their bodies are no longer able to do. Conversely, a person's body may function well but he or she is limited by changes to his or her mental health or memory. After the discussion, tell the learners that they will make puppets and develop, practice, and present a puppet show to help them understand some of the things elderly people experience as forms of imprisonment. Assign one of the challenges that impacts the elderly to individuals or small groups.

Demonstrate the steps for making a soft sculpture rod puppet. Invite the students to follow along and pause to offer assistance as needed. Provide nylon stocking pieces, fiberfill, and paper towel tubes. Tie a knot in one end of a piece of nylon. Put a small amount of stuffing in the bottom of the nylon pouch. Place a paper towel tube in the center of the stuffing and add more fiberfill until the stocking is full enough to stretch the sides of the nylon. Tie a small strip of nylon around the opening to secure the stocking to the paper tube.

Provide pins, needles, and thread and show everyone how to move the stuffing around to create facial features. Pin the facial features in place and then use a needle and thread to sew the folds and puffs in the puppet head. Remove the straight pins when this step is completed.

Set out crayons, markers, or makeup, glue, scissors, and felt scraps. Use the crayons, markers, or make-up to shade the cheeks or areas around the eyes and mouth. Cut eyes and a mouth from felt scraps and glue them in place. If desired, plastic eyes could be used and glued to the head to create more movement.

Create hair using yarn, additional fiberfill, or fake fur and offer these supplies to the puppet makers. Cut and temporarily pin the hair in place on the top of the head. Stitch or glue to the nylon and then remove the pins.

Distribute the foam rubber pieces and tell the group that they will form arms with this material. Cut a slit in the center of the foam rubber and slide it up the paper tube to the bottom of the head. Cut the ends of the foam into the shape of hands or glue or sew fabric hands onto the ends of the foam.

As the last step, supply fabric pieces for clothing. Drape the material over the shoulders and around the neck. It can be slid up the tube by removing and replacing the puppet's arms. Sew or glue the costume in place

Once the soft sculpture rod puppets are completed, instruct the creators to use them by holding the paper tube and moving the character to suggest the action.

If the stage was not prepared ahead of time, involve the group in constructing it at this point. The directions are provided in the Advance Preparation section.

Allow time for the individuals or groups to prepare and practice their presentations. Remind them that each person or team will do a short scene, based on the assigned problem, showing how elderly people may feel imprisoned. Take turns presenting the scenes in the stage. After each puppet show, talk about people the students may know who experience the situation which was presented. Discuss ways in which the participants can help people who are imprisoned in that way. Suggestions might include read to a person with poor eyesight, provide a ride for someone without a driver's license, or visit a family member, friend, or neighbor who is alone due to the death of a spouse. Prompt each participant to be more aware of the needs of older people and to consider ways to help meet these challenges.

Conclude the session by reading Psalm 46:1 to the group. Remind them that God promises to be with us through all of life's situations.

Reading about Addictions

Psalm 142:7

Bring me out of prison,
so that I may give thanks to your name.
The righteous will surround me,
for you will deal bountifully with me.

Learn

Participants will hold a Read-a-Thon to learn about addictions that imprison people.

Locate

► Beverages, meals, and snacks (optional)

► Bible

► Books, brochures, comics, journals, and magazines on addictions appropriate for the age of the group

► Copy machine or printer

► Dictionary

► Glasses, napkins, plates, and silverware for meals and refreshments (optional)

► Information on addiction prevention and recovery organizations

► Notebooks

► Paper for copy machine or printer

► Pencils or pens

► Resource sheet: "Read-a-Thon Sponsor Sheet"

Advance Preparation

► Determine the topics to be covered in the session based on the age of the participants.

► Designate a non-profit ministry or organization involved in prevention or rehabilitation of one of the addictions to receive the funds collected during the Read-a-Thon.

► Duplicate the "Read-a-Thon Sponsor Sheet" for each participant.

► Enlist chaperones to monitor the event.

► Recruit pledges for segments of time books are read.

Lead

Addictions are a form of imprisonment experienced by people of all ages. Babies are born addicted to drugs, children experiment with cigarettes and often become addicted to nicotine, young people try alcohol because of peer pressure and sometimes become alcoholics, and adults suffer from addictions to food, caffeine, gambling, and many other things. Psalm 142:7 says "Bring me out of my prison, so that I may give thanks to your name." One way to help people avoid the imprisonment of addiction is by learning more about the issues. This activity provides suggestions for holding a Read-a-Thon to help young people discover more about addictions which can imprison.

Look up the word addiction in a dictionary. It means "to give oneself up to a strong habit." In other words, it means to become imprisoned by a substance such as drugs or alcohol or an activity like gambling or overeating. Learning about addictions that imprison people can be done through many formats. Interesting, informative printed materials are available from a variety of sources. Books, as well as magazines, journals, brochures, and comics, are published for people of all ages, with topics ranging from family situations to faith subjects. Hold a Read-a-Thon as a way to educate people about addictions that imprison people. Designate a time and a place where materials will be read continuously. Begin on a Friday evening, and run non-stop through Saturday night, or hold the event for one day, or for specific hours of a day. The event can occur in the group's regular meeting place in a church or school or at the home of a leader or a participant. Those involved need to commit to be present at certain times and to engage in reading about addictions while there.

Preparations for the event are vital and must be done in various ways several weeks before the event. At one meeting with the group, explain the idea. If part of the purpose of the Read-a-Thon is to raise funds for a ministry or an organization that serves addicted people, prepare sponsor sheets and distribute them to the participants. Challenge the group to find people who will pledge money for each fifteen minute segment of the event. Gather books from various sources but also ask each participant to collect three separate resources about addictions and bring them to the gathering. Instruct everyone to bring a notebook and pen or pencil to the Read-a-Thon to record information about the materials they read. People should also

be asked to bring pillows, sleeping bags, and snacks, if appropriate. Inform adult chaperons of the schedule and ask them to be present at designated times.

At the beginning of the Read-a-Thon, gather the group and explain the policies and procedures. Each person must keep track in his or her notebook of the books read and the amount of time spent reading. They should also make notes on the information they learn. Encourage everyone to keep reading until the time runs out, stopping only for munching snacks, eating meals, stretching limbs, and taking bathroom breaks. If varying age groups are involved, assign people to designated rooms.

If desired, incorporate special events throughout the Read-a-Thon. For example, invite local authors, media personalities, and church or school personnel to read during a fifteen minute segment; use a time slot to read a book to the entire group; and have adults read to children and young people read to adults for part of the time.

At the conclusion of the event, allow the participants to share the information they learned about the imprisonments caused by addictions.

Instruct the participants to contact their sponsors, collect the pledges, and return the money to a designated person by a specific date. Arrange to send the money to the selected agency.

At another time, hold a Film-a-Thon to share additional information about addictions that imprison.

Read-a-Thon Sponsor Sheet

Dear Sponsors,

We the _____ group are sponsoring a Read-a-Thon to better inform ourselves on the many issues connected with addictions to things like alcohol, drugs, food, and gambling.

I am asking you to pledge a donation for the time I have promised to read. All the collected funds will be donated to: _____.

You will be contacted after the event takes place on _____ so that you may make your donation. Thank you very much.

Sincerely,

_____

      I agree to pledge the following amount for each fifteen minutes of reading:

  Name of Sponsor:

Contact Information:

Pledge (per 15 minutes):

    Signature:

Touching with Love

Matthew 8:3

He stretched out his hand and touched him, saying, 'I do choose. Be made clean!' Immediately his leprosy was cleansed.

Learn

Participants will use music and movement to remember people who need Jesus' healing touch because of imprisonment through health conditions.

Locate

- Bibles
- Cards, 3" x 5"
- Copy machine or printer
- Envelopes
- Equipment to play music
- Equipment to project images of hands (optional)
- Music for "Healing Hands" by Elton John (YouTube)
- Music for "By Your Touch" by Jaime Rickert (YouTube)
- Paper for copy machine or printer
- Pens
- Pictures of hands (optional)
- Resource sheet: "Jesus' Touch Scripture Verses"
- Scissors
- Screen (optional)

Advance Preparation

- If desired, find or take photos of people using their hands to touch or help others.
- If photos are used, practice projecting and coordinating the pictures of hands with the selected background music.
- Write one word of each of the following Bible verses on an index card or duplicate and cut apart the words of the verses on the Jesus' Touch resource sheet. Place the cards or the words for each verse in a separate envelope. Verses to use include:
  - Matthew 8:3 - Healing the leper
  - Matthew 8:15 - Healing Peter's mother-in-law
  - Mark 5:41 - Healing Jarius' daughter
  - Mark 10:16 - Jesus blesses the children
  - John 9:6 - Healing the man born blind
- Be aware that, due to a variety of circumstances, some people might be uncomfortable holding hands with others in the group. Before beginning the music, explain that an action during the song will be to reach out and hold or touch another person's hand. State that anyone who does not wish to participate may leave his or her hands at their side or extend them overhead.

Lead

In the New Testament there are many stories of ways in which Jesus used his hands to touch people, both to heal them and to show them his care and concern. Jesus touched not only lepers but people who were blind, ill with fever, paralyzed, and possessed by demons. All of these were people who were imprisoned within their own bodies. Today there are also many people with physical, mental, and emotional illnesses who are imprisoned in the same way and who can benefit from the gift of touch. Use this music and movement activity as a way to explore the theme of touching others with the healing love of Jesus.

Invite the participants to review scripture passages that illustrate Jesus' attitudes and actions on this theme. Explain that the words of selected verses have been written on separate index cards and that they must be put in order before they can be read. Organize the participants into five small groups and give one envelope to each team. Remind the learners that their challenge is to put the words together in the proper order to form the verse. Once they think the words are in sequence, they may take a Bible and check their work. Provide time for the pupils to complete this portion of the activity. Once everyone is ready, allow time for one or more participants from each group to share their passage and to talk about what Jesus' actions meant to the person in need.

Talk with the students about people today who need a loving touch. Mention that there are many types of imprisonment and suggest that one way is being trapped inside one's own body due to a health related condition. Offer examples such as persons with Alzheimer's Disease, individuals infected with HIV or AIDS, and people afflicted with other physically handicapping conditions. Often people imprisoned in their own bodies are viewed as untouchable and unlovable, and because of this people are afraid to come into physical contact with them. But they, like everyone, need a healing hand to touch both their hearts and their bodies. Invite the students to share their thoughts and feelings related to reaching out and touching these folks. Since Jesus is no longer on the earth, ask the group who can provide this important physical contact. Of course, the answer is people who love Jesus and who want to share Jesus' love with others.

Play a song that expresses a message of love through the sharing of a warm embrace or a loving touch. "Healing Hands" by Elton John or "By Your Touch" by Jaime Rickert are good examples. Ask the pupils to listen carefully and thoughtfully to the words. Play the song again and invite the group to add gestures to the music, reaching their hands out to one another at the appropriate times.

After the song, encourage the participants to express what it felt like to reach out and to take hold of another person's hand. Discuss ways in which this can be done on a regular basis, especially in relation to people who are imprisoned within their own bodies. If possible, make plans to visit a hospital or a nursing home and share the music and gestural interpretation with the residents who need a special touch of Jesus' love.

If desired, enhance the experience by showing pictures of people using their hands to touch or help others. Coordinate the visual presentation with the words of the selected song.

Conclude the activity by asking the group to repeat phrases of the following prayer and to recite it together:

Lord Jesus, you reached out to touch and to heal people whom others shunned. Help us to follow your example by reaching out to all who are imprisoned in their own bodies, that through us they may feel your love and know the power of your healing. Amen.

Jesus' Touch Scripture Verses

Matthew 8:3 - Healing the leper

He stretched out his hand and touched him, saying, 'I do choose. Be made clean!' Immediately his leprosy was cleansed.

Matthew 8:15 - Healing Peter's Mother-in-law

He touched her hand, and the fever left her, and she got up and began to serve him.

Mark 5:41 - Healing Jarius' daughter

He took her by the hand and said to her, 'Talitha cum,' which means, 'Little girl, get up!'

Mark 10:16 - Jesus blesses the children

And he took them up in his arms, laid his hands on them, and blessed them.

John 9:6 - Healing the man born blind

When he had said this, he spat on the ground and made mud with the saliva and spread the mud on the man's eyes.

Feeling Trapped by Abuse

Zechariah 9:12
Return to your stronghold,
O prisoners of hope; today I declare that
I will restore to you double.

Learn

Participants will create a weaving as they review ways to remember people who have experienced abuse.

Locate

- ► Bible
- ► Cardboard for loom
- ► Copy machine or printer
- ► Cord, ribbon, or string
- ► Fabric, solid colors
- ► Markers
- ► Paper for copy machine or printer
- ► Resource sheet: "Helping Someone Imprisoned by Abuse"
- ► Scissors
- ► Tape, duct

Advance Preparation

- ► Copy the Helping Someone Imprisoned by Abuse resource sheet. Cut the page into strips along the dotted lines.
- ► Cut fabric into strips two inches wide and four to five inches longer than the width of the loom.
- ► Make a large loom for weaving. Cut a piece of cardboard at least two feet by two feet. Along the top and bottom edge, cut a

one inch slit every two inches. Using cord, yarn, or ribbon string the loom. Start at the top left corner. Tie the cord in a knot between the end of the cardboard and the first slit. Tape the end of the cord firmly to the back of the cardboard, using duct tape to secure it. Pull the cord into the first slit. Then string it to the bottom of the cardboard, pulling it into the bottom slit. Stretch the cord to the next bottom slit and pull it to the front of the loom. String the cord to the matching slit at the top. Repeat this pattern until the entire loom has been strung. Tape the end of the cord firmly in place, knotting it around the end of the loom for added security.

- ► Arrange for a professional, such as a counselor, who deals with issues of abuse, to be involved in this presentation. In addition, use this lesson in conjunction with other Safe Environment sessions.

Lead

A person who has been abused may be imprisoned by anger, fear, and sadness as a child, youth, or adult. Sometimes the abuse hurts so much that the person blocks it from memory. When this happens part of the person is imprisoned within and the abuse is locked away as a dark secret. People who are or have been abused often feel separated from others because of the secret they hide. Of course, it is important for anyone who has been abused to receive the proper physical, mental, emotional, and spiritual support so that they can feel whole again. In this activity the students will learn more about this topic and share their concern for those who have been abused as they work together to create a weaving of fabric and words that will be used to pray for others.

Begin the lesson by telling the group that some children, as well as people of all ages, experience abuse. Some types of abuse may be emotional, mental, physical, sexual, and verbal. Explain that often this means that someone hurts another person's body or mind or touches them in a way that harms or scares them. Ask group members to share what they have heard or know about abuse from news reports, television programs, or school information sessions. Correct any misunderstanding the participants may have about abuse.

Then read Zechariah 9:12. "Return, you exiles who now have hope; return to your place of safety. Now I tell you that I will repay you twice over with blessing for all you have suffered." (*Good News Translation*) Explain that exiles are people who have been sent away and are held like prisoners in another country. Point out that in this verse the prisoners are being offered freedom, hope, and safety. Ask the students to name things which might help a person who has been abused to feel these blessings. Also ask what others can do to help the abused person recover from, or be freed of, the things which he or she has experienced. Distribute the slips of paper, prepared in advance, to individuals and small groups. Note that the word on each paper is an example of a way to help someone who has been abused. Provide time for the learners to read the word and the

explanation on the paper they received. Then invite volunteers to take turns sharing the ideas and explanations outlined on the cards.

Tell the group that they will work together to create a weaving of these words as a symbolic prayer prompter to help them remember people who are abused. Give each person a strip of cloth and a marker. If the group is large, two or three students can work together on the same strip. If it is small, each student should be given two pieces of paper and cloth. Each person or group should write the word on the piece of cloth. When this part of the project is completed, invite each individual or small group to take turns showing the strip, telling what it means, and weaving it into the loom. If several people on a team share a word strip, make sure everyone gets an opportunity to weave it into the loom, or give the others an additional strip on which to write the same word, or offer blank pieces of cloth so that everyone can add a piece of fabric to the weaving.

When the weaving is completed, give each person an additional strip of cloth. Form a circle, with every two people holding a strip of cloth in their hands between them. Place the completed weaving in the middle of the circle. End the activity with a shared prayer. Direct each person or team to slowly name the word they wove into the loom. After all the words have been spoken, the leader or group can conclude the prayer by saying, "Help us to weave these things into the lives of those who have been abused, helping to free them and to create for them a beautiful future. Amen."

Helping Someone Imprisoned by Abuse

Accepting

People who have been abused need to feel accepted by others. Often they feel bad or damaged and blame themselves for what happened.

Believing

Sometimes a person tells someone else about the abuse and they are not believed. Then the individual feels helpless and hopeless. It is important to believe the person.

Caring

Showing a loving attitude and acting in kind ways toward someone who has been abused helps him or her to understand that not everyone will hurt them like the person by whom they were harmed.

Empathizing

This means to try to put oneself in the place of the other person. When people attempt to understand others in this way, it helps them to be more caring and helpful.

Laughing

Laughter can be very healing. Having fun can help a person to feel better and to enjoy life again.

Listening

Listening is one of the best gifts a person can give to another person. Allowing people to talk about feelings can help them to heal from their sadness or anger. It is hard, but important, to listen without interrupting or giving the person advice.

Praying

Pray for the people who have experienced abuse. Also pray for all people who are sad and hurting because of this experience in their lives.

Protecting

If someone is being actively abused, it is important to help them find safety. Responding is one way of protecting the person. Going with them to tell a responsible adult is another.

Responding

If told about abuse, it is important to tell someone who can help the person who is being abused. Share the information with a parent, teacher, principal, pastor, priest, or other responsible adult. If that person does not respond, tell someone else.

Supporting

Healing takes time. People who have been abused may feel their hurt for a long period. Although the abuse may have taken place long ago, offer support by offering the caring and listening they need during the long healing process.

Sympathizing

Sometimes people who have been abused need someone who will allow them to cry or who will cry with them. Showing grief is an important part of the healing process.

Understanding

People who have been abused need to know that others understand them. It is important to comprehend why individuals act or respond with anger, distance, fear, or sadness.

BIBLIOGRAPHY

Hungry

Currie, Robin and Debbie Trafton O'Neal. *Hunger Ideas for Children.* Chicago, IL: Evangelical Lutheran Church In America, 1991.

Editors. *About World Hunger.* South Deerfield, MA: Channing L. Bete, 1987.

Hampson, Tom, Sandi McFadden, Phyllis Wezeman, and Loretta Whalen. *Make a World of Difference: Creative Ideas for Global Learning.* New York: Friendship Press, 1989.

Miller, J. Keith. *A Hunger for Healing.* San Francisco: Harper, 1991.

Office on Global Education, Church World Service and Center for Teaching International Relations, University of Denver. *Children Hungering for Justice - Grades K-4, 5-8, and 9-12.* Washington, DC: U.S. Committee for World Food Day, N.D.

Rupp, Joyce. *Fresh Bread and Other Gifts of Spiritual Nourishment.* Notre Dame, IN: Ave Maria Press, 1985.

Wezeman, Phyllis Vos and Jude Dennis Fournier. *Connections, Choices & Commitments: A Youth Retreat about Hunger.* Elkhart, IN: Church World Service, 1990.

Thirsty

Editors. *Let's Learn about Using Water Wisely.* South Deerfield, MA: Channing L. Bete, 1988.

-----. Water Conservation. *A Coloring & Activities Book.* South Deerfield, MA: Channing L. Bete, 1984.

-----. *Water: Our Most Valuable Resource.* South Deerfield, MA: Channing L. Bete, 1985.

Harris, D. Mark. *Embracing the Earth: Choices for Environmentally Sound Living.* Chicago, IL: Noble Press, 1990.

Hays, Edward. *Prayers for a Planetary Pilgrim.* Easton, KS: Forest of Peace Books, 1988.

Wiessner, Colleen Aalsburg and Phyllis Vos Wezeman. *The Flavors of Faith.* Brea, CA: Educational Ministries, Inc., 1990.

Wiessner, Colleen Aalsburg. *Singing Mountains and Clapping Trees.* Grandville, MI: Reformed Church Press, 1991.

Stranger

Fry-Miller, Kathleen M., Judith A. Myers-Walls, and Janet R. Domer-Shank. *Peace Works. Young Peacemakers Project Book II.* Elgin, IL: Brethren Press, 1989.

Liechty, Anna L., Phyllis Vos Wezeman, and Judith Harris Chase. *Festival of Faith: A Vacation Church School Curriculum Celebrating the Gifts of God.* Prescott, AZ: Educational Ministries, Inc., 1993.

Mains, Karen Burton. *Open Heart, Open Home.* Elgin, IL: David C. Cook, 1976.

Mummert, J. Ronald with Jeff Bach. *Refugee Ministry in the Local Congregation.* Scottdale, PA: Herald Press, 1992.

Wezeman, Phyllis Vos. *Peacemaking Creatively through the Arts.* Brea, CA: Educational Ministries, Inc., 1990.

Wezeman, Phyllis Vos and Jude Dennis Fournier. *Joy to the World.* Notre Dame, IN: Ave Maria Press, 1992.

Wezeman, Phyllis Vos and Kenneth R. Wezeman. *Missions: 52 Creative Methods for Teaching Christ's Message.* Prescott, AZ: Educational Ministries, Inc., 1993.

Poor

Caes, David. *Caring for the Least of These.* Scottdale, PA: Herald Press, 1992.

Cunningham, Frank J., Editor. *Words to Love by... Mother Teresa.* Notre Dame, IN: Ave Maria Press, 1988.

Grady, Duane. *Helping the Homeless. God's Word in Action.* Elgin, IL: Brethren Press, 1988.

Kenyon, Thomas L. with Justine Blau. *What You Can Do to Help the Homeless.* New York: Simon & Schuster, 1991.

Schlabach, Gerald W. *And Who Is My Neighbor? Poverty, Privilege, and the Gospel of Christ.* Scottdale, PA: Herald Press, 1990.

Wezeman, Phyllis Vos and Colleen Aalsburg Wiessner. *Gleanings from Ruth.* Brea, CA: Educational Ministries, Inc., 1988.

Wezeman, Phyllis Vos and Colleen Aalsburg Wiessner. *Benjamin Brody's Backyard Bag.* Elgin, IL: Brethren Press, 1991.

Sick

Archdiocese of Saint Paul-Minneapolis. *The Many Faces of Jesus, Matthew 25.* Dubuque, IA: Brown Publishing-ROA Media, 1989.

Eisentrout, Virginia A. *The Healthy Life: A Biblical Approach.* New York: United Church Press, 1989.

Hamma, Robert M. *Come to Me: Prayers In Times of Illness.* Notre Dame, IN: Ave Maria Press, 1993.

Raber, Ann. *Congregational Wellness Course.* Goshen, IN: Mennonite Mutual Aid, 1987.

Travis, John W. and Regina Sara Ryan. *Wellness Workbook.* Berkeley, CA: Ten Speed Press, 1988.

Wezeman, Phyllis Vos. *Through the Heart: Creative Methods of HIV & AIDS Education.* Leeds, MA: Leader Resources, 2011.

Yancey, Philip. *Where Is God When It Hurts?* Grand Rapids, MI: Zondervan, 1977.

Imprisoned

Colson, Charles. *Born Again.* Grand Rapids, MI: Baker Book House, 1976.

Dychtwald, Ken and Joe Flower. *Age Wave: The Challenges and Opportunities of an Aging America.* Los Angeles: Jeremy P. Tarcher, Inc., 1989.

Feldmeth, Joann Ross and Midge Wallace Finley. *We Weep for Ourselves and Our Children.* San Francisco, CA: Harper, 1990.

Peck, M. Scott. *The Road Less Traveled: A New Psychology of Love, Traditional Values & Spiritual Growth.* New York: Simon & Schuster, 1978.

Washton, Arnold M. and Donna Boundy. *Willpower's Not Enough: Recovering from Addictions of Every Kind.* New York: Harper Collins, 1989.

Yost, Don. *Waiting on the Outside.* Goshen, IN: Bridgework Theater, 1983.

Zehr, Howard. *Changing Lenses: A New Focus for Crime and Justice.* Scottdale, PA: Herald Press, 1990.

RESOURCES

Two children's books by Phyllis Vos Wezeman to use with these lessons:

Benjamin Brody's Backyard Bag

Phyllis Vos Wezeman and Colleen Aalsburg Wiessner

Chris Raschka, Illustrator

Elgin, IL: Brethren Press, 1991

Benjamin's playful experiment to find how many things he can do with an empty paper bag leads him to an informative encounter with a bag lady who has no home of her own.

Written for children in lower elementary grades, this colorful and delightfully illustrated book will capture the interest of all ages. It carries a poignant message for families about creating solutions to help the homeless.

Petra's Pier Picnic

Phyllis Vos Wezeman, Author and Oscar Joyo, Illustrator

Chicago, IL: ACTA Publications, 2018

Petra's Pier Picnic is a simple story of birthday gifts, a fishing trip, and a family meal that addresses the complex topic of hunger as Petra watches her two fish interact, discovers there are people in need, and decides to share. Written for children in lower elementary grades, this vibrantly illustrated book will capture the interest of all ages. It includes practical suggestions to help families address hunger issues.

Both available from:

The Pastoral Center
844-727-8672
resources@pastoralcenter.com
http://pastoral.center

METHODS

Architecture

Walls	I Was Imprisoned	Breaking Down Walls

Art

Bread Symbols/Actions	I Was Hungry	Spreading the Word
Cartoons	I Was Poor	Helping the Homeless
Chalk Mural	I Was Thirsty	Appreciating Water
Clay Cup	I Was Thirsty	Filling a Cup in Jesus' Name
Collage	I Was Imprisoned	Overcoming the Bonds of Materialism
Cooperative Cartoon	I Was Sick	Portraying Health Issues
Cut Outs/Prayers	I Was Hungry	Caring through Prayer
Fabric Stitched Card	I Was Sick	Sending a Caring Message
Graffiti Wall	I Was a Stranger	Putting Out the Welcome Mat
Love Mobile	I Was a Stranger	Singing the Language of Love
Origami Cup	I Was Thirsty	Quenching a Thirst
Pennant	I Was Sick	Ministering in Mercy
Pin Punched Paper Heart Decoration	I Was a Stranger	Welcoming New Neighbors
Poster (Prayer Marathon)	I Was Sick	Uplifting the Sick
Poster (Sun Rays)	I Was Imprisoned	Spreading Some Sunshine
P-R-A-Y-ing Hands	I Was a Stranger	Offering a Prayer
Sponge Print Card	I Was Thirsty	Thirsting for God
Three-D Display on Water Themes	I Was Thirsty	Praising God for Water
Welcome Wreath	I Was a Stranger	Displaying Hospitality
Wooden Spoon	I Was Hungry	Remembering the Hungry
Woven Mat	I Was Poor	Addressing Unemployment Issues

Banners/Textiles

Brown Paper Bag Banner	I Was Hungry	Working for Justice
Patchwork Banner or Quilt	I Was Poor	Responding to Needs
Pocket Banner	I Was Sick	Taking Care of the Sick
Rag Doll	I Was Poor	Clothing the Poor
Weaving	I Was Imprisoned	Feeling Trapped by Abuse

Creative Writing

A-Z Poems/Prayers	I Was Thirsty	Praising God for Water
Acrostic Poem	I Was a Stranger	Offering a Prayer
Acrostic Poem	I Was a Stranger	Putting Out the Welcome Mat
Fairy Tales	I Was Hungry	Dispelling the Myths
Five Word Poems	I Was Thirsty	Appreciating Water
Healing Prayer	I Was Sick	Focusing on Feelings
Journal	I Was Sick	Identifying the Feelings
Letters	I Was Imprisoned	Suffering for Their Beliefs
Letters	I Was Sick	Ministering in Mercy
Litany	I Was Hungry	Spreading the Word
Litany	I Was Thirsty	Flowing with Justice
Picture Booklet	I Was Thirsty	Living Water
Poems of Lament	I Was Poor	Expressing the Pain
Prayer Marathon	I Was Sick	Uplifting the Sick
Public Service Announcement	I Was Sick	Proclaiming the Message
Recipes for Healthy Living	I Was Sick	Creating Recipes for Healthy Living
Word Web	I Was Sick	Portraying Health Issues

Culinary

Breads of the World	I Was Hungry	Spreading the Word
Cupcakes	I Was Poor	Celebrating the Caring
Pretzels/Water	I Was Thirsty	Thirsting for God

Dance/Gesture/Movement

Friendship Song	I Was a Stranger	Making New Friends
Gestural Interpretation	I Was Hungry	Recognizing the Hungry
Gestural Interpretation	I Was Imprisoned	Touching with Love

Drama

Care and Care-less Skit	I Was Thirsty	Quenching a Thirst
Freeze Frame	I Was Sick	Focusing on Feelings
Improvisation	I Was a Stranger	Talking at Home
Mime	I Was Sick	Identifying the Feelings
Monologues	I Was Poor	Becoming Personally Involved
Talk Show	I Was Hungry	Hungering for Happiness

Games

Bags/Objects	I Was Thirsty	Refreshing Water Themes
Biblical Situation Cards	I Was Hungry	Setting the Example
Buckets/Ten Categories	I Was Thirsty	Discovering Water Facts
Concentration – Crime Fighters	I Was Imprisoned	Unlocking the Fears
Contemporary Situation Cards	I Was Hungry	Setting the Example
Go Fish	I Was Sick	Meeting Special Needs
Matching Emotion/Illness	I Was Sick	Focusing on Feelings
Maze/Obstacle Course	I Was Imprisoned	Overcoming the Bonds of Materialism
Puddle Hop	I Was Thirsty	Thirsting for God
Riddles	I Was a Stranger	Blessing a Stranger
Scavenger Hunt	I Was Poor	Searching for Support

Scrambled Words	I Was Imprisoned	Learning about Literacy
Tray of Objects	I Was Thirsty	Exploring Pollution Problems
World of Welcome Matching Game	I Was a Stranger	Engaging Others

Music

Friendship Song	I Was a Stranger	Making New Friends
Listen to Lyrics	I Was Poor	Encouraging through Music
Listen/Play/Write Songs	I Was Thirsty	Refreshing Water Themes
Song: "By Your Touch"	I Was Imprisoned	Touching with Love
Song: "Healing Hands"	I Was Imprisoned	Touching with Love
Song: "I Was Hungry"	I Was Hungry	Recognizing the Hungry
Song: "Love In Any Language"	I Was a Stranger	Singing the Language of Love
Song: "The Tree Song"	I Was Thirsty	Thirsting for God
Song to "Row, Row, Your Boat"	I Was Imprisoned	Learning about Literacy

Photography

Film - "Martin the Cobbler"	I Was a Stranger	Showing Kindness to All
Picture Booklet	I Was Thirsty	Living Water
Pictures – Hands	I Was Imprisoned	Touching with Love
Pictures – Items/Crime	I Was Imprisoned	Unlocking the Fears

Puppetry

Balloon Rod Puppet	I Was Thirsty	Exploring Pollution Problems
Bottle Rod Puppet	I Was Poor	Giving for the Poor
Brown Paper Grocery Bag Body Puppet	I Was Sick	Sharing Your Resources
Paper Tube Rod Puppet	I Was Sick	Proclaiming the Message
Plastic Tub Rod Puppet	I Was a Stranger	Showing Kindness to All
Soft Sculpture Rod Puppet	I Was Imprisoned	Hiding in a Secret Prison

Storytelling

Biographies	I Was Imprisoned	Suffering for Their Beliefs
Book – *Benjamin Brody's Backyard Bag*	I Was Poor	Helping the Homeless
Book – *Cobbler Martin*	I Was a Stranger	Showing Kindness to All
First Person Stories	I Was Poor	Becoming Personally Involved
Folktale – "The Rabbit In the Moon"	I Was Hungry	Sharing Your Resources
Read-a-Thon	I Was a Imprisoned	Reading about Addictions
Rhythm Story: "Multiplying the Food"	I Was Hungry	Multiplying the Food
Storytelling: Feed My Sheep	I Was a Stranger	Caring through Prayer
"Where Love Is, God Is"	I Was a Stranger	Showing Kindness to All

SCRIPTURE

Scripture: Old Testament

Genesis 1:1-2; 9-10	I Was Thirsty	Living Water
Genesis 1:1-10	I Was Thirsty	Appreciating Water
Genesis 1:29-31	I Was Hungry	Setting the Example
Genesis 5:1-9:17	I Was Thirsty	Discovering Water Facts
Genesis 18:1-8	I Was Hungry	Setting the Example
Genesis 18:1-10	I Was a Stranger	Blessing a Stranger
Genesis 19:1-3	I Was a Stranger	Engaging Others
Genesis 24:43-46	I Was Thirsty	Quenching a Thirst
Genesis 29:9-20	I Was a Stranger	Blessing a Stranger
Genesis 45:16-24	I Was Hungry	Setting the Example
Genesis 47:13-17	I Was Hungry	Setting the Example
Exodus 13:3-10	I Was Hungry	Setting the Example
Exodus 14:1-21	I Was Thirsty	Discovering Water Facts
Exodus 15:23	I Was Thirsty	Exploring Pollution Problems
Exodus 16:4-35	I Was Hungry	Overview
Deuteronomy 8:7-9	I Was Thirsty	Living Water
Ruth 2	I Was Poor	Overview
Ruth 2	I Was a Stranger	Offering a Prayer
Ruth 2:1-16	I Was Hungry	Setting the Example
2 Samuel 9	I Was Hungry	Setting the Example
1 Kings 4:1-7	I Was Poor	Overview
1 Kings 17:7-16	I Was Poor	Overview
1 Kings 17:8-16	I Was Hungry	Setting the Example
1 Kings 17:8-16	I Was a Stranger	Blessing a Stranger
1 Kings 19:1-15	I Was Hungry	Setting the Example

2 Kings 4:8-17	I Was a Stranger	Blessing a Stranger
2 Kings 4:42-44	I Was Hungry	Setting the Example
Psalm 1:1-3	I Was Thirsty	Living Water
Psalm 1:3	I Was Thirsty	Refreshing Water Themes
Psalm 1 – Psalm 7	I Was Poor	Expressing the Pain
Psalm 23	I Was Sick	Uplifting the Sick
Psalm 23:1-2	I Was Thirsty	Living Water
Psalm 25	I Was Poor	Expressing the Pain
Psalm 25:16	I Was Sick	Sending a Caring Message
Psalm 41:1-2a	I Was Thirsty	Living Water
Psalm 42:1-2	I Was Thirsty	Thirsting for God
Psalm 46	I Was Sick	Uplifting the Sick
Psalm 46:1	I Was Imprisoned	Hiding in a Secret Prison
Psalm 65:9-10	I Was Thirsty	Living Water; Praising God for Water
Psalm 90:17	I Was Poor	Addressing Unemployment Issues
Psalm 100:5	I Was Sick	Proclaiming the Message
Psalm 103:1-5	I Was Sick	Uplifting the Sick
Psalm 107:10	I Was Imprisoned	Unlocking the Fears
Psalm 118:4-5	I Was Sick	Uplifting the Sick
Psalm 139:7-14	I Was Sick	Uplifting the Sick
Psalm 142:7	I Was Imprisoned	Reading about Addictions
Psalm 146:7	I Was Hungry	Working for Justice
Ecclesiastes 4:14	I Was Imprisoned	Learning about Literacy
Isaiah 35:5-7	I Was Thirsty	Living Water
Isaiah 40:30-31	I Was Sick	Uplifting the Sick
Isaiah 41:17	I Was Thirsty	Discovering Water Facts
Isaiah 41:17-20	I Was Thirsty	Living Water
Isaiah 43:1-3a	I Was Sick	Uplifting the Sick
Isaiah 55:1	I Was Hungry	Overview

Isaiah 58:7	I Was Poor	Helping the Homeless
Isaiah 58:10	I Was Hungry	Recognizing the Hungry
Isaiah 58:11	I Was Thirsty	Living Water
Isaiah 61:1	I Was Imprisoned	Overview
Jeremiah 17:7-8	I Was Thirsty	Thirsting for God
Jeremiah 29:11-13	I Was Sick	Uplifting the Sick
Daniel 1:8-17	I Was Hungry	Setting the Example
Amos 5:24	I Was Thirsty	Flowing with Justice
Jonah 1-2	I Was Thirsty	Discovering Water Facts
Zechariah 9:12	I Was Imprisoned	Feeling Trapped by Abuse

Scripture: New Testament

Matthew 3:11	I Was Thirsty	Living Water
Matthew 3:17	I Was Thirsty	Discovering Water Facts
Matthew 5:3	I Was Poor	Overview
Matthew 5:4	I Was Sick	Identifying the Feelings
Matthew 5:6	I Was Hungry	Hungering for Happiness
Matthew 5:6	I Was Thirsty	Thirsting for God
Matthew 5:7	I Was Sick	Ministering In Mercy
Matthew 5:10-12	I Was Imprisoned	Suffering for Their Beliefs
Matthew 6:11	I Was Hungry	Remembering the Hungry
Matthew 6:34-44	I Was Hungry	Overview
Matthew 8:3	I Was Imprisoned	Touching with Love
Matthew 8:14-15	I Was Hungry	Setting the Example
Matthew 8:15	I Was Imprisoned	Touching with Love
Matthew 12:1-8	I Was Hungry	Dispelling the Myths
Matthew 12:1-8	I Was Hungry	Setting the Example
Matthew 14:13-21	I Was Hungry	Multiplying the Food
Matthew 22:36-40	I Was a Stranger	Singing the Language of Love

Matthew 25	I Was Poor	Encouraging through Music
Matthew 25:35-40	I Was Hungry	Setting the Example
Matthew 25:35-45	I Was Hungry	Recognizing the Hungry
Matthew 25:35a, 36b, 37a, 42a, 44a	I Was Hungry	Overview
Matthew 25:35b, 37b, 42b, 44a	I Was Thirsty	Overview
Matthew 25:35c, 38a, 43a, 44a	I Was a Stranger	Overview
Matthew 25:36a, 38b, 43b, 44b	I Was Poor	Overview
Matthew 25:36b	I Was Sick	Taking Care of the Sick
Matthew 25:36b, 39a, 43c, 44b	I Was Sick	Overview
Matthew 25:36c, 39b, 43c, 44a	I Was Imprisoned	Overview
Matthew 25:40	I Was Hungry	Overview
Matthew 26:17-29	I Was Hungry	Setting the Example
Mark 5:41	I Was Imprisoned	Touching with Love
Mark 6:31-55	I Was Hungry	Multiplying the Food
Mark 9:41	I Was Thirsty	Filling a Cup in Jesus' Name
Mark 10:16	I Was Imprisoned	Touching with Love
Mark 12:41-44	I Was Poor	Giving for the Poor
Luke 1:26-38	I Was a Stranger	Blessing a Stranger
Luke 4:18-21	I Was Sick	Uplifting the Sick
Luke 6:30-31	I Was Poor	Celebrating the Caring
Luke 9:12-17	I Was Hungry	Multiplying the Food
Luke 10:25-37	I Was Sick	Portraying Health Issues
Luke 10:29-37	I Was Hungry	Setting the Example
Luke 12:15-21	I Was Hungry	Setting the Example
Luke 12:34	I Was Imprisoned	Overcoming the Bonds of Materialism
Luke 14:15-21	I Was Hungry	Setting the Example
Luke 15:11-32	I Was a Stranger	Talking at Home
Luke 16:19-31	I Was Hungry	Setting the Example; Spreading the Word
John 2:1-11	I Was Thirsty	Discovering Water Facts

John 4:7-15	I Was Thirsty	Living Water
John 6:1-14	I Was Hungry	Multiplying the Food; Setting the Example
John 7:37-38	I Was Thirsty	Living Water
John 9:6	I Was Imprisoned	Touching with Love
John 11:17-44	I Was a Stranger	Blessing a Stranger
John 12:8a	I Was Poor	Overview
John 13:3-5	I Was Thirsty	Living Water
John 15:13	I Was Hungry	Sharing Your Resources
John 21:4-14	I Was Hungry	Setting the Example
John 21:4-18	I Was Hungry	Caring through Prayer
Acts 2:43-47	I Was Hungry	Setting the Example
Acts 6:1-7	I Was Hungry	Setting the Example
Acts 6:5	I Was Poor	Becoming Personally Involved
Acts 9:26-28	I Was a Stranger	Making New Friends
Acts 9:36-41	I Was Poor	Clothing the Poor
Acts 11:19-26	I Was a Stranger	Making New Friends
Acts 16:11-15	I Was Hungry	Setting the Example
Acts 16:11-15	I Was a Stranger	Blessing a Stranger
Acts 16:13-15	I Was a Stranger	Putting Out the Welcome Mat
Acts 16:16-40	I Was Imprisoned	Suffering for Their Beliefs
Romans 12:13	I Was a Stranger	Welcoming New Neighbors
Romans 15:25, 26	I Was Poor	Responding to Needs
1 Corinthians 6:19	I Was Sick	Creating Recipes for Healthy Living
Ephesians 2:14	I Was Imprisoned	Breaking Down Walls
Philippians 1:12-13	I Was Imprisoned	Suffering for Their Beliefs
Philippians 4:4-8	I Was Sick	Focusing on Feelings
1 Thessalonians 5:11	I Was Poor	Encouraging through Music
1 Timothy 3:2	I Was a Stranger	Overview
Titus 1:8	I Was a Stranger	Overview

Hebrews 12:1	I Was Sick	Meeting Special Needs
Hebrews 13:2	I Was a Stranger	Showing Kindness to All
Hebrews 13:3	I Was Imprisoned	Spreading Some Sunshine
James 2:14-17	I Was Hungry	Setting the Example
James 2:14-17	I Was Poor	Searching for Support
James 5:13-14	I Was Sick	Uplifting the Sick
1 Peter 4:9-10	I Was a Stranger	Displaying Hospitality
1 John 4:7-11	I Was a Stranger	Singing the Language of Love
Revelation 7:15-17	I Was Thirsty	Living Water

ABOUT THE AUTHOR

Phyllis Vos Wezeman

As a religious educator, Phyllis Wezeman has served as Director of Christian Nurture at a downtown congregation in South Bend, Indiana, Executive Director of the Parish Resource Center of Michiana, and Program Coordinator for ecumenical as well as interfaith organizations in Indiana and Michigan.

In academics, Phyllis has been Adjunct Faculty in the Education Department at Indiana University South Bend and in the Department of Theology at the University of Notre Dame. She is an "Honorary Professor" of the Saint Petersburg (Russia) State University of Pedagogical Art where she has taught methods courses for extended periods on several occasions. She has also been guest lecturer at the Shanghai Teachers College in China.

As founder of the not-for-profit Malawi Matters, Inc., she develops and directs HIV & AIDS Education programs with thousands of volunteers in 200 villages and more than 1,000 schools in Malawi, Africa including "Creative Methods of HIV & AIDS Education," "Culture & HIV-AIDS," and "Equipping Women/Empowering Girls."

Author or co-author of over 1,950 articles and books, she has written for over 80 publishers.

Phyllis served as President of Active Learning Associates, Inc.; a consultant or board member to numerous local and national organizations such as the American Bible Society, Church World Service, LOGOS, and the Peace Child Foundation; leader of a six-week youth exchange program to Russia and the Ukraine; and Project Director for four Lilley Worship Renewal grants. She is the recipient of three "Distinguished Alumni Awards" and recipient of the Aggiornamento Award from the Catholic Library Association.

Wezeman holds undergraduate degrees in Business, Communications, and General Studies from various institutions and an MS in Education from Indiana University South Bend.

Phyllis and her husband Ken (who met when they were in second and third grade in elementary school) have three children and their spouses, Stephanie (Jeff), David, and Paul (Deha), five grandchildren, Quin, Ayle, Lief, Ashley (Mike), and Jacob, and two great-grandsons, Maddox and Troy.

MORE ENGAGING RESOURCES BY
phyllis vos wezeman

⬇ DOWNLOADABLE 📑 REPRODUCIBLE ↪ SHARABLE 🏷 AFFORDABLE

52 Interactive Bible Stories

A Collection of Action, Echo, Rhythm, and Syllable Stories

Participants will love these playful ways of expressing Scripture.

74 PAGES • 8½"x11"
DOWNLOADABLE: $14
PAPERBACK + DOWNLOAD: $19.80

100 Creative Techniques for Teaching Bible Stories

A treasure chest of fun ideas and activities, split across ten categories, for bringing Scripture to life.

108 PAGES • 8½"x11"
DOWNLOADABLE: $14
PAPERBACK + DOWNLOAD: $19.80

Experience the Saints • 4 Volumes
Activities for Multiple Intelligences

Eight activities per saint, each based on a different learning intelligence. Includes whole family and general classroom guides, with reproducible handouts.

- Vol. 1: Patrick, James, Hildegard of Bingen • PW201
- Vol. 2: Francis, Clare, Margaret of Scotland • PW202
- Vol. 3: Joan of Arc, Thomas Becket, Agnes • PW203
- Vol. 4: Peter, Catherine of Siena, Scholastica • PW204

200 PAGES PER VOLUME • 8½"x11"
$14 PER VOLUME • $42 FOR ALL 4 (SAVE 25%)

Praying by Number
Creative Prayer Lessons & Activities

- Two volumes, with 20 activities each.
- Fun and faith-filled ways to teach children and families how to talk to God.

76 PAGES PER VOLUME • 8½"x11"
DOWNLOADABLE: $16 EA.
PAPERBACK + DOWNLOAD: $21.60 EA.

Seasons by Step: A Week-by-Week Thematic Approach

Use these creative approaches to explore a theme in-depth over the course of a season through Scripture. Each includes **talking points for children's messages, at-home family activities, artwork** for weekly symbols, and more.

Know Chocolate for Lent *(Lent & Holy Week)*

Uses the growing and manufacturing process of chocolate as a metaphor for the growth of faith and discipleship in the Christian life. Adult formation materials for a parish-wide approach are sold separately.

80 PAGES • LR119 • $18

God's Family Tree *(Lent & Holy Week)*
Tracing the Story of Salvation

Tells the story of God's people as they struggle to find faith and hope for life through the symbols of trees found in Scripture. Includes optional Easter pageant and classroom activities.

114 PAGES • LR116 • $18

In the Name of the Master *(Advent/Christmas/Epiphany)*
Sharing the Story of Christ

Uses a variation of the Advent wreath that uses fruits as symbols for the many names of God's Masterpiece, Jesus. Help your kids & families go deeper as they light their Advent candles each week.

37 PAGES • LR108 • $14

⬇ DOWNLOADABLE   ◈ REPRODUCIBLE   ↪ SHARABLE   ⌁ AFFORDABLE

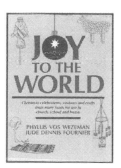

Joy to the World
International Christmas Crafts & Customs

Dozens of activities, from 12 countries that you can use again and again. Develop an appreciation for the contributions of the peoples of all lands and races to the celebration of Christmas

DOWNLOAD • 159 PAGES • 8½"x11"
LR104 • $18

Ideas A-Z
Crafts & Activities for Advent, Christmas, & Epiphany

Offers different theme or learning approach for each letter of the alphabet. Great ideas for intergenerational activities, lesson plans, or worship experiences.

PAPERBACK BOOK • 94 PAGES • 8½"x11"
PW102 • $11

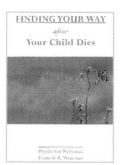

Finding Your Way after Your Child Dies

Offers parents a comforting way to grieve. Easily adapted for use in small and large group settings such as a support group, prayer service, or family ministry session.

PAPERBACK BOOK • 192 PAGES
IC937005 • $14.95

http://pastoral.center/phyllis-vos-wezeman

 The Pastoral Center   *Pastoral ministers serving pastoral ministers*

---

http://pastoral.center • resources@pastoralcenter.com • Call us at 844-727-8672 (M-F 9am-5pm CT)

Made in the USA
Monee, IL
26 January 2021